ORDER FROM CHAOS

Harness Your Potential.
Reshape Your World - A 40-Day Journey

By,

G. Lan Ijiwola, Ph.D.

Summit House
Publishers

Chicago

Copyright © 2016 by Gregory Ijiwola
Paperback ISBN: 978-1-7356699-3-9

All rights reserved. No part of this publication may be reproduced, distributed, or transmitted in any form or by any means, including photocopying, recording, or other electronic or mechanical methods, without the prior written permission of the publisher, except in the case of brief quotations embodied in critical reviews and certain other non-commercial uses permitted by copyright law.

Unless otherwise indicated, Scripture quotations are from The ESV® Bible (The Holy Bible, English Standard Version®),
copyright © 2001 by Crossway, a publishing ministry of Good News Publishers. Used by permission. All rights reserved.

Scripture quotations marked (NLT) are taken from the Holy Bible, New Living Translation, copyright ©1996, 2004, 2015 by Tyndale House Foundation. Used by permission of Tyndale House Publishers, Carol Stream, Illinois 60188. All rights reserved.

Scripture quotations marked MSG are taken from THE MESSAGE, copyright © 1993, 1994, 1995, 1996, 2000, 2001, 2002 by Eugene H. Peterson. Used by permission of NavPress. All rights reserved. Represented by Tyndale House Publishers, Inc.

Scripture quotations marked (NIV) are taken from the Holy Bible, New International Version®, NIV®. Copyright © 1973, 1978, 1984, 2011 by Biblica, Inc.TM Used by permission of Zondervan. All rights reserved worldwide. www.zondervan.com

Printed in the United States of America

CONTENTS

1. Knowing God 1
2. How Things Start 5
3. The God Of Power 8
4. Something Out Of Nothing 11
5. Order Out Of Chaos 15
6. Words Rule 19
7. What Exactly Do You Want? 23
8. Evening Comes Before Morning 26
9. One Day At A Time 29
10. A Giant Womb 33
11. The Hidden Future In Now 36
12. A Briefer History Of Time 40
13. Variety Is The Spice 44
14. Primary Purpose 48
15. Secondary Purpose 52
16. Be Fruitful And Multiply 56
17. Seed Consciousness 59
18. Premium Food 62
19. God Is Good 66
20. Holy Time 70
21. Natural Habitat 74

22. A Revelation Of Work 77
23. Power To Choose 82
24. Learning To Say No 86
25. Consequences 91
26. Partnership 95
27. Bone Of My Bones 98
28. The Anatomy Of Temptation 102
29. The Good News 107
30. Take Responsibility 111
31. Two Forces 115
32. Is This The Best I Can Do? 121
33. Brother's Keeper 125
34. A Higher Realm 129
35. The Favor Of God 132
36. Persistent Faith 135
37. Maranatha 138
38. Seasons Of Life 142
39. You Have A Covenant With God 146
40. Possibilities In Unity 151

ACKNOWLEDGMENTS

I want to thank all the people who were regular readers and commenters on *Beginning with God Devotionals* when I was posting them on my blog and on social media. Your encouragement and comments gave me the impetus I needed to continue writing, which led to this book.

Special thanks to my wife, Debo, and my children Jesse, Josh, and Pearl for consistently creating a great atmosphere at home that allows me to write, and for your support in writing this volume and my other writing projects.

INTRODUCTION

It is interesting to note that the books that piqued my interest in this genre of writing were not religious. I remember reading some of Isaac Asimov's collections of essays on various subjects and being so intrigued by how he expounded on these subjects, some very complex, in a straightforward, humorous, and entertaining way.

Then I read "A Brief History of Time" by Stephen Hawking which used a similar approach to explaining complex scientific thoughts to laymen. I wondered why the atheists were having all the fun.

Then a friend gave me C.S Lewis's collection of works for one of my birthdays, and I also got into Max Lucado's books. They were so enlightening.

Then I felt the pull, which I believe is from God, to start writing essays in the form of daily discourses on Scripture verses starting from the book of Genesis. I began writing and posting some of these thoughts on my online blog, Beginning with God Devotionals, and I was surprised at the interest people showed in them. People were visiting the blog from different parts of the world and interacting with the posts.

The decision was made later to collect these essays, write more, and put them in books, of which this one is the first. That was how this book was born.

In this volume, I share thoughts on several key verses in the first 11 chapters of Genesis. These discourses are expository in nature but with a keen focus on making them very practical and actionable for you as you read them.

The best way to get the most out of this book is to follow the daily reading format. Start by reading the biblical anchor text at the top, meditate on it and then read the following commentary. This volume focuses on learning from the divine principles in the first section of Genesis and then using them to order our world and harness our potential for God's glory.

I pray that this book will be of tremendous blessing to you. If it is, please pass it on.

G. Lan Ijiwola, Ph.D.
C.E.O, The Life Development Center.

| DAY 1

KNOWING GOD

"In the beginning, God created the heavens and the earth."

- Genesis 1:1

When, our kids, were younger, I fielded questions from them regularly. Questions like, "Who made the world?" "Why did God create the world?" "What does God look like?" "Where does God live?" "Why did the dinosaurs die? Why can't we see God?" "Does God sleep or eat?" and more.

I think the innocent questions of kids prove that to ask questions is beautifully human. It is how we were made. We are inquirers by nature. I have also come to believe that providing answers is a divine pleasure. It seems the cosmos is arranged to inspire questions and make seekers out of us.

Starting from our text today, the Book of Genesis answers many questions about God and existence. This initial sentence of the Bible is pregnant with truth first, that the universe has not always existed but has a beginning, and second, that it was created out of nothing by an entity called God.

Of these two facts from the verse, it is popularly accepted that the universe had a beginning in the event scientists call the Big Bang, but there are different opinions on what or who this First Cause is. Who is this person or thing who brought all that is seen and unseen into existence? The Bible calls Him God.

A survey of various beliefs shows the differing conceptions of God:

    1. The Atheist says He doesn't exist.

    2. The Agnostic says that even if He exists, we cannot know anything about Him.

Even among those who believe in His existence, there are differing views:

    1. Some see Him as a celestial policeman looking for an opportunity to mete out punishment on erring human beings

    2. Some perceive Him as a powerful malevolent being who sends tornadoes, earthquakes, and hurricanes destroying everything in His path, as you would see in an insurance company's policy on "Acts of God."

    3. Some, like Deists, see Him as an extremely intelligent and powerful Being who created the

universe but is no longer in contact with it and doesn't respond to people's prayers.

4. The Pantheists see him as a powerful impersonal force that permeates the universe and is part of nature.

5. The Polytheists say many gods and deities are superintending in shared rulership, the various parts of existence.

However, we shouldn't have to guess. God has made Himself known to those who deny His existence and those who believe He exists and wants to know His nature and attributes.

To those who deny His existence, He has made Himself known through the beauty, harmony, intricacy, and order of the universe and nature and innately through their conscience (Psalm 19:1-6, Romans 1:18-21). And to those who believe in His existence, He has made His nature and attributes known to them through His word, the Bible.

Where do you stand today? Do you want to know this magnificent being who created you and the universe and your purpose in the scheme of things? According to the Bible, He wants you to know Him. He is eager to reveal Himself to you.

Your very first step in knowing him is to ask Him to reveal himself to you and then begin to read your Bible systematically. Also, savor the majestic beauty of nature and God's handiwork and let them remind you of His greatness and power. Doing this could be the best decision you would ever make.

Decision of the Day

God wants me to know Him and has revealed Himself, His nature, and attributes through the work of His hands in nature and the Bible. I am going on a quest to know Him intimately. I will begin to study my Bible prayerfully and systematically, expecting to know Him more and more.

| DAY 2

HOW THINGS START

"In the beginning, God created the heavens and the earth."

- Genesis 1:1

I happen to be one of those late entrants in popular TV series. I recall watching *Game of Thrones* a couple of weeks before its grand finale. However, being late into the game did not eliminate my obsession with sequence. What comes first must always come first. We must never cheat order and logic, especially in movies, or the world falls apart!

Enters the fantastic but guilt-inducing and time-wasting exercise called binging. I must know how it all began. So, I started from the beginning. At least I didn't have to wait several seasons over many years to know when winter would finally come, but I got to know how it all began.

In the Hebrew Bible, the Book of Genesis is named *B'rêshîth*. This is from the first word in our text today. It speaks of the beginning, not of the beginning as in eternity, but of the start of the Creative Week (literal or figurative) soon expounded in the following verses of Genesis 1.

Later in the Bible, John begins his book using a similar phraseology but with a different meaning of an eternal past (John 1:1).

Stretching the *Game of Thrones* analogy (We just must make things work!), Genesis 1:1 was not speaking of the life of the beginning of the existence of the director or producer of the series, in this case, God, creating the heavens and the earth, but of the beginning of the making of the movie. God transcends creation just as the movie director exists before the movie and transcends it.

God has no beginning. He is eternal, stretching forward and backward to infinity. Alpha and Omega. First and Last. He was. He is. He is to come (Rev 22:13). He began the beginning and started the start.

Everything that we see in the cosmos, and some we don't see, had a beginning - a first cause. Their scripts were written, the sets were put up, the actors put in place, and the movie commenced. Behind it, all was the Director. He is whom we call God. He was responsible for it all.

Tucked in this verse is one of the primary lessons of creating divine order from the chaos of our lives: order must be ordered, and new beginnings must be begun. Someone must take responsibility for directing the movie. If the book must be written, the author has to say "yes" and get to work.

ORDER FROM CHAOS

As Newton said, every object remains in a state of rest or uniform motion unless compelled by an external force to act otherwise. Nothing moves until they are moved.

Take responsibility for your life, the good, the bad, and the ugly. Assume the position of the director under God. Blame no one. Make no excuses. Begin authoring a new story. This is how you unleash the creative power for a new beginning.

Decision of the Day

I understand that just as God took up the task of creation at the beginning if I must reorder my life, I must take responsibility. I must assume the place of director of my life under God. I, therefore, choose today to retake my power to create change by letting go of all blame and excuses.

| DAY 3

THE GOD OF POWER

"In the beginning, God created the heavens and the earth."

- Genesis 1:1

Once, a boy flying to visit his grandparents sat beside a man who was a seminary professor. The professor saw the boy was reading a take-home paper from Sunday school. So, he thought of having some fun with the boy. "Young man," the professor said, "if you can tell me something God can do, I will give you this big apple."

The boy was quiet for a couple of seconds, thinking, then he responded, "Sir if you can tell me something God can't do, I'll give you a whole box of apples!"

Smart boy! Our text today is, again, the very first sentence of the Bible, and it speaks to this great truth about God - He is a God of great power who can do all things.

The Hebrew word translated as "God" here is the word *Elohim*. The root word "El" means "strength" or "power," so *Elohim* is "The Strong One" or "The Powerful One." It

ORDER FROM CHAOS

speaks of a mighty being with incomparable strength and power. He displayed this power when He created the whole universe out of nothing. Therefore, one of the first revelations of God to you in His word about Himself is concerning His strength and power.

Life brings many situations and circumstances that we cannot handle with our limited human abilities: seemingly impossible dreams and goals such as a doctor's report of a terminal disease. There are impossible financial situations, the salvation of a loved one that seems unlikely as the days pass, a habit that has proved impossible for you to quit, or a disintegrating marriage that seems to defy all cures.

What all these require is a higher power. God possesses the ability to do what is impossible to man. There is no impossibility with Him. He can change every situation you face without breaking a sweat. If you put your trust in Elohim, the God of creation, the same power that created the world out of nothing is available to you.

Are you feeling tired or weary about life? Do you think you've run out of gas? You don't have to stay there. He is the God who gives power to the weak and strength to those who have no might. Those who wait on Him will renew their strength, and they will be able to soar like eagles (Isaiah 40:30-31).

So today, refuse to accept the human word as final. Don't let the situations you face weigh you down. Call upon Him in a whisper. Commit your future into His able hands.

ORDER FROM CHAOS

Entrust your life's burdens to Him. He knows what to do with them.

Decision of the Day

God has revealed Himself to me as the "Strong One." While my strength is weak and limited, His is perfect. I look to Him for strength in my weaknesses. I consciously commit all the seemingly impossible situations of my life into His hands. I trust that He knows what to do with them.

| DAY 4
SOMETHING OUT OF NOTHING

"In the beginning, God created the heavens and the earth."

- Genesis 1:1

So, you blew it.
It was the opportunity of a lifetime, but you froze. You couldn't deliver. Now it's gone.
You let down those who trusted you. Now, they are gone.
Or maybe you didn't mess up. You just can't see a way out of the mess life has become lately.
Great ideas, but no movement. Big dreams, but no capital.
Just an:

    Empty heart after the breakup,

    Empty room after the divorce,

    Empty church after the split,

    Empty house after the loss of a loved one,

    Empty womb, after countless fertility treatments,

    Empty bank account despite working several jobs.

Emptiness, A.K.A: void, nothingness, blankness, hollowness, vacuum, loss of all, depletedness, desertedness, destitution, is the state of containing nothing, having nothing, and lacking substance.

But what does our text today have to do with emptiness? Yesterday, we saw the revelation of God as the strong and powerful One in this verse. This is, however, not the final disclosure of God about Himself in this verse. God also reveals Himself as the Creator God who can bring something out of nothing.

According to Hebrews 11:3-4, the vastness of creation was fashioned from things that do not exist. Just think about it and savor the awesomeness. The whole earth and all the billions of stars and galaxies were created from nothing.

Nothing was there, and suddenly, everything was there! Job says he hung the earth on nothing (Job 26:7). This is an excellent testimony to the fact that God is not intimidated or hindered in His purpose by the absence of materials. All He needs is Himself. He is All-sufficient.

ORDER FROM CHAOS

In looking to God for any sort of intervention, you may be tempted to look around and conclude that there is nothing for God to work with.

You may have a business idea but lack the capital or a massive vision with no wherewithal to accomplish it. It might be the absence of opportunities, a worthy spouse, a job, credibility, experience, wisdom, capability, courage, or health.

Whatever you lack, just remember that the absence of things does not stop God from fulfilling His purpose in your life. He can make a grand creation from the raw material of no raw materials. Emptiness is no deterrent to His works in your life. God is all God needs to accomplish His works. God is all you need too. In Him is everything and from Him proceeds all you need in life. He is your righteousness, capital, opportunity, experience, wisdom, and capability. He's your all in all. He's all you will ever need. Do not be afraid of anything.

So, face today with unwavering faith. Confront the lack in your life with joy and laughter. Speak to the dry bones and the quiet, stony cemetery of your life with the confidence of faith, knowing that your God can raise an army out of dry bones (Ezekiel 37), children out of stones (Luke 3:8), and your future out of nothing. All He wants is your dependence on Him—and even that only happens by His grace.

Decision of the Day

    I understand that my lack does not hinder God's work in my life. He has no shortage in Himself, and He is my sufficiency. Even though I look around me now, and I am confronted with the absence of many things I need for my life and purpose, I know that it is ultimately not things I need but God Himself who is the source of all things. So, I will look to Him in faith, trusting His grace is sufficient for me.

| DAY 5

ORDER OUT OF CHAOS

"And the earth was without form and void, and darkness was upon the face of the deep. And the Spirit of God moved upon the face of the waters."

- Genesis 1:2

" Hello, I am the Holy Spirit, and I am pleased to meet you! This Book, which you call the Bible, is my work. I inspired it and would like to introduce myself to you early on in it because you will see me a lot in this book and need me to understand it. Is there a better way to introduce myself to you than for you to see me doing what I do best, working alongside Elohim to create life, order, and beauty out of chaos?"

Immediately after Elohim was introduced as the Creator and Powerful One, we are immediately introduced to another individual in the Godhead. Today, we meet the Holy Spirit. Our first introduction to Him tells us a lot about His work.

First, we see Him operating on earth when it was dark, empty, and without form. It was in chaos. He began to move upon the empty watery waste. The word "moved" in the Hebrew language means to "flutter," "vibrate," or "brood." The Spirit of God was brooding over the waste like a hen would brood over her eggs in preparation for the hatching of new life. This is significant. The Holy Spirit is introduced as the one who directly painted the empty canvas of the earth with color and beauty and brought order out of chaos in partnership with Elohim.

In other parts of scripture, we see the Holy Spirit operating similarly. He came upon people and empowered them (Judges 3:10), He overshadowed Mary, and she became pregnant with the Savior (Luke 1:35). He came in like a rushing wind on Pentecost. He turned timid men into bold, unrelenting world changers (Acts 2). He moved upon simple men, and they produced the Holy Writ, the Bible (2 Peter 1:21). The Holy Spirit is still the same. He never changes. He is still moving upon people, circumstances, and places.

Think about the description of the state of the earth when the Spirit began to move on it. Isn't this an accurate description of the way anything is before God begins to move on it? Empty, dark, and chaotic. Is this a description of any aspect of your life right now? Do you feel your life is a wasteland of unfulfilled dreams, broken promises, and unattainable goals?

ORDER FROM CHAOS

Are you hurting from a visit by the hurricane of life that has smashed down almost everything you felt was standing and sure? Are you enjoying your walk with God, or is it just a daily drudgery, a dull routine you struggle to keep up with? Is your zeal for God still white-hot, or has your faith boiled down to just fire insurance to ensure that you do not end up in hell?

Could you do with a new burst of inspiration, a new dosage of joy, a renewed vision, a rejuvenated body, or a more passionate faith? A fresh encounter with the Holy Spirit will do this and more in your life.

Ask God today to fill you afresh with the Spirit. Ask Him to reveal in your life the Great Comforter. Ask Him to fill every room of your house with His presence. Ask Him to inspire you again and empower you for your tasks. Invite Him to begin hovering over your circumstances as He did at the beginning.

Go to places where you see Him moving. Associate with people whose lives you see Him moving upon. Get under His influence. He will bring order out of chaos, victory out of defeat, and today you can start living that vibrant, joyful, creative, and powerful life your heart so desires.

Decision of the Day

I open my life to the Holy Spirit. I invite Him to fill every part of it with His renewing presence. I acknowledge

ORDER FROM CHAOS

my dependence on Him, my total powerlessness without Him. I will expose my life to His influence through every means possible. I invite Him to saturate my environment and circumstances with His glorious presence.

| DAY 6

WORDS RULE

"And God said, let there be light: and there was light."

- Genesis 1:3

In his book, *Politics*, the ancient Greek philosopher Aristotle wrote about the concept of the Rule of Law. This is a principle that everyone within a nation, state, or community of people should be held to the same standard –the law, and that it should be enforced equally all the time, irrespective of person or status. This has become the espoused judicial philosophy of many nations, including the United States (even though the application is still imperfect).

In thinking about today's text, I was also reminded that the natural order of the universe is regulated and maintained by laws (Job 38:33, Jeremiah 33:25). Chief of these laws is the one revealed in our text today—the Rule of Words.

In the following few verses of Genesis, God gives us a glimpse into how He does things. He reveals to us His method of creation and renewal. From verses 3 to 29, the phrase "God said" is repeated over and over. God is revealed as a God who uses His words to accomplish things. He discloses Himself as a speaking God. He created, illuminated, ordered, separated, blessed, and named all creations using His words' instrumentality.

What is the significance of this? First, it lets us know that God's method of creation and accomplishing things is through speaking. His words are the tools He uses in creating and sustaining creation. Hebrews 1:3 says, "He controls and sustains everything by his word of power." Isaiah 54:10-12 and Psalm 107:20 make it known that God uses His words with purpose, sending them forth as messengers on various errands, and they never return to Him without fulfilling their assignments.

Even when He wanted to send His Son into the world, He sent Him as the Living Word, who came to dwell among us gloriously (John 1). The Son also came into the world and lived like the Father. He healed the sick, cast out devils, calmed raging seas, commanded trees, and raised the dead with His words.

Second, our text lets us know the place of words in the scheme of things. Words rule. Everything was made from words, so everything is controlled by words. Even now, we see that words are in abundance on earth. They fill the airwaves. They exist in written and visual forms. Words live on (John 6:63). They linger on years after they are spoken, even when the speakers are long gone, either in the memories of the hearers, in records, or in the atmosphere they are spoken into.

They wound or heal, convey love, or hate, make or break, raise or raze. They are vehicles carrying either life or death (Proverbs 18:21). They can foster peace or incite wars. They can inspire people to outstanding accomplishments or immobilize them with fear. It depends on how they are used.

Granted, your words are not at the same level as God's words, but knowing the place of words in the scheme of things and knowing you are created in the image of God to function like Him, how are you going to use words? How have you been using them?

Do you speak without purpose, letting words drip out of your mouth without considering the effects they are causing on others and your circumstances? Did you know that you are bound by the consequences of the words you speak (Proverbs 6:2)? Did you know that there is a corresponding judgment for every idle (non-working, purposeless) word you say? (Matthew 12:36). Did you know that what surrounds you in life now is partly because of how you have been speaking?

Your words are so crucial that your salvation is left to what you believe and say about the redemptive work of Jesus (Romans 10:9-10).

Today you have a choice to change your life, to put away perverse speech, and imitate your heavenly Father by speaking living, creative, loving, and productive words.

Honor His Word in the Bible. Meditate on them and make them your own. Ask Him to help you tame your tongue.

Obey the Rule of Words. If you do this consistently, everything around you will soon begin to change. A beautiful Eden can come out of the chaos and darkness of your life.

Decision of the Day

I know that God is a speaking God who uses words productively. Jesus also showed me by His example the correct use of words. I am created in God's image. I am commanded to imitate my Father (Ephesians 5:1) and to follow the example of Christ. Today I will do away with perverse and purposeless speech. I will meditate on God's words and begin to align my speech to conform with them to the glory of His name.

| DAY 7

WHAT EXACTLY DO YOU WANT?

"And God said, "Let there be light," and there was light. ⁴ And God saw that the light was good. And God separated the light from the darkness.

- Genesis 1:3-4

In his book, The Fourth Dimension, David Yongii Cho, who was the pastor of the largest church in the world, shared an important principle of faith—being specific in prayer. He wrote about a time he lived in a small room, eating, studying, and sleeping on the floor because he had no bed, desk, or chair. He also had to walk several miles to carry out his ministry because he had no other means of transportation.

In reading the Bible, he learned that he was a child of God, the King of kings and that if he asked God to meet his needs, God would answer him. So, he prayed and asked God for a bed, chair, desk, and bicycle.

However, months passed after his prayers, and he received nothing. He was so discouraged that he wept and complained to God about his unanswered prayers.

While he was weeping, he heard the Spirit of God speak to him, telling him that the problem was that his prayers were so vague that it was impossible to be answered. They were not specific, so his faith could not lay hold of them. Cho immediately corrected his prayer by asking for a chair made by Mitsubishi with rollers, a desk made from Philippine mahogany, and an American-made bicycle with gears on the side, describing them with greater specificity.

Shortly afterward, he received those things, precisely all he had requested. He said he learned from that time that God does not answer vague prayers. He wants us to be specific when we ask things of him. We should let him know with clarity what we truly desire. Pastor Cho used this faith principle to build the largest church in the world by asking God for a specific number of people per time and standing in faith until he received them in the church.

In our text today and throughout the first chapter of Genesis, we see God exemplifying the same principle of faith. He was particular about what he desired to create. He called on light and described in detail how dry land should separate from the waters, how plants, marine animals, and land-based animals should be formed with seeds in them, and even human beings were to be formed in his image and likeness. He was direct and specific. He had a clear-cut picture in his mind of what he intended to see created.

Jesus Christ also showed adherence to this principle when he would ask those who came to him for help what they would want him to do for them exactly (Mark 10:51). He also taught this principle in Mark 11:24 as he spoke to his disciples about prayer.

If specificity in faith is important to Jesus, then you should learn to practice the same. In prayer, go beyond just asking God to do things for you in generalities. Instead of asking God to bless you, tell him exactly what you desire in your life.

This is the reason why keeping a prayer journal is beneficial. Using the journal, you can write down things you desire from God in specific terms. Write down the answer to Jesus' question in Mark 10:51, "What do you want me to do for you?" do this for the various aspects of your life, and you will soon see these things manifest all around you to your joy and God's glory.

Decision of the Day

I understand that I must be specific in praying to God for my needs. I must have a clear-cut picture of the things I am asking God for such that I can describe them beyond generalities. I choose today to make this part of my prayer life and to keep a prayer journal where these requests are recorded and crossed off as they manifest in my life.

| DAY 8

EVENING COMES BEFORE MORNING

"God called the light Day, and the darkness he called Night. And there was evening and there was morning, the first day.

- Genesis 1:5

If you are like me and most of the world, you think of the day as starting in the morning and ending in the evening—dawn to dusk. Well, it looks like we got it wrong. We have it in reverse (just as we tend to arrange other things out of God's original order—a recipe for chaos in our lives).

Our text today indicates that from the time of creation, a day was initially delineated as evening followed by morning. The Jewish people kept this pattern until the time of Jesus, and some devout Jews keep it until today. For example, for the Jews, the Sabbath starts on Friday evening, not Saturday morning. A day's fasting starts from dusk to dusk. According to the law of Moses, when someone touches a dead body, they are unclean till evening, just before the start of another day.

ORDER FROM CHAOS

Check out these passages.

"It shall be to you a Sabbath of solemn rest, and you shall afflict yourselves. On the ninth day of the month beginning at evening, from evening to evening shall you keep your Sabbath."

Lev 23:32

"And he said to me, "For 2,300 evenings and mornings. Then the sanctuary shall be restored to its rightful state."

Daniel 8:14

"Ok, I get it," you say, "so the Jews believed the day started in the evening, but what does that have to do with me now living in a world that sees the day in the reverse order?"

Well, I am not trying to get you to sleep in the morning and wake up in the evening to start your day and then rock it through the night before going to bed in the morning. We can pull some essential things from this creative order to help bring order out of chaos in our lives.

First, the Hebrew word for "evening" in our text does mean evening, darkness, night, or sunset. Still, it derives from the concepts of chaos, blackness, mixture, disorderliness, obscurity, and lack of visibility.

The evening is symbolic of decreased visibility, chaos, and increasing disorder.

On the other hand, the word for "morning" is the exact opposite and speaks of brightness, visibility, and increased order. So, in the original order of the day, there is a progression from chaos to order, obscurity to visibility, and darkness to light.

This is so powerful and prophetic! It speaks of the desired progression of God for our lives—from chaos to order, sin to righteousness, weeping to joy, curses to blessing, selfishness to love, depression to delight, mourning to dancing. No wonder the psalmist exclaimed, "Weeping may tarry for the night, but joy comes in the morning... You have turned my mourning into dancing..." (Psalm 30:5,11) and "the path of the righteous is like the light of dawn, which shines brighter and brighter until full day" (Provers 4:18).

Receive this message today. You are on a journey from evening to morning in this divine order of your life. It gets better, brighter, and clearer. As you present your life to God, you are being transformed into his image through the daily renewal of your mind. Order is coming into your chaos. It's a new day! Good evening and great morning!

Decision of the Day

I now see the divine spiritual progression of my life from evening to morning. Things are getting better, brighter, and clearer. I am moving from chaos to increasing order and conformity to God's image. I accept this perspective to life from this day and make it my own by faith.

| DAY 9

ONE DAY AT A TIME

"And God said, "Let there be an expanse in the midst of the waters, and let it separate the waters from the waters." ^{7} And God made the expanse and separated the waters that were under the expanse from the waters that were above the expanse. And it was so. ^{8} And God called the expanse Heaven^j And there was evening and there was morning, the second day.

- Genesis 1:6-8

It happened. Once, a rich man promised his son that he would give him an allowance once a year. So, every year on the same day, he would give his son the lump sum amount for the year. After some time, the son only came to see the father once a year on the day of the allowance. So, the father changed things up by only giving the son enough funding for a day. The next day the son showed up and began to show up daily from then on.

ORDER FROM CHAOS

Of course, this is a fictitious story by an unknown author. I like it because it illustrates the thought for our meditation today.

Today's text shows a movement forward in the Creative Week to the second day. Reading on in the chapter, we see how creation unfolded day by day until the culmination with the creation of humanity on the sixth day.

I understand that there is some disagreement among genuine people on whether these were literal days or figurative days representing long periods. This does take from the central truth that creation was not accomplished in one fell swoop but a progressive version over a period.

But why did God not create everything all at once, even though He had the power to do so but chose to do it in this progressive manner? Could this be a pattern with God He is trying to show us from the very first pages of the Bible about his M.O? Is he Father 1.0 in our story who gave lump sums to use or Father 2.0 who operated using a more frequent daily allowance schedule?

Reading through the first chapter, we can say convincingly that He is indeed a process God. He can do everything all at once, but He chooses to chunk it into more minor aspects as he did in creation. So, day one was light, day two was the firmament, day three the dry land, and so on, even at the creation of mankind. Rather than immediately populating the earth, he chose to make two humans who would, through a process, eventually become billions of people on the planet.

ORDER FROM CHAOS

Later we would see that He allowed Israel to gather only a day's worth of manna and not more, except for the Sabbath day when they could pick two-day's worth. Jesus would teach us to pray," Give us this day our daily bread." (Matt 6:11), and to not worry about tomorrow because tomorrow would take care of itself (Matt 6:33, 34).

Today's goal is to learn to think long-term but to act in the short term. Think big but live life one day at a time. Complete your projects in chunks. Eat the elephant of your vision one bite at a time. Don't worry about firmament while you are still in the phase of creating light. Confer with God daily to see what he has provided and planned for the day, and then dive into each day with gusto.

Perhaps like the father in our story, God planned it this way so we would never be far from His presence because our success depends on our daily conference and his help recreating our lives after the divine order. Perhaps it is to keep us walking by faith and not by sight when His plans are not microwaved but cooked. Perhaps each step in the process is to enhance our capacity and preparedness for the next.

Whatever the reason, God gave us insight into the way he does things in Genesis 1. He introduced Himself as the God of the process; since we are made in his image, we should imitate him.

Decision of the Day

I understand that God is a God of process. He showed me how He works by creating sequentially and breaking the

ORDER FROM CHAOS

operation over six days. I will imitate him by having a long-term view but breaking my overall goals into chunks of steps that lead to my overall vision. I will take little steps of faith each day. In this process, I will learn to wait on Him and abide in his presence.

| DAY 10

A GIANT WOMB

"And God said, "Let the earth sprout vegetation, plants yielding seed, and fruit trees bearing fruit in which is their seed, each according to its kind, on the earth." And it was so. ¹² The earth brought forth vegetation, plants yielding seed according to their own kinds, and trees bearing fruit in which is their seed, each according to its kind. And God saw that it was good.

- Genesis 1:11-12

I have always been intrigued by farming. I learned a lot about life watching plants sprout. I took lessons on patience, resilience, and nurturing from planting crops.

Growing up in Africa, I was involved in farming at various levels. It started in the garden beside our house, where we planted legumes, corn, and vegetables, then it advanced to accompanying my dad during visits to large-scale cocoa farms owned by my grandfather. At school, each student had to take responsibility for a portion of land where we were to cultivate certain food crops. Now, living in the United States, I continue my lessons with plants nurturing grass, trees, evergreens, and vegetable gardens in the backyard.

From my first planting exercise, digging the soil, inserting some bean seeds, and watching them sprout within three days, I began to see the cultivation of plants as a miracle and the earth as the conduit of this miraculous power.

Later as I began to learn more about how life works, I realized that this miraculous ability to take a seed, bring new life out of it, and cause it to sprout and produce, extends beyond the ground but to every domain on planet earth (think of words as seeds that grow in hearts, deeds that boomerang back to the doers, smiles begetting smiles, emotions generating emotions after their kind when expressed, and so on).

Also, several scripture passages mention the law of seeding and harvesting (Gen. 8:20-22, Luke 6:37-38, Gal 6:7, Mark 4:26-29). I began to refer to the earth as a giant womb.

This giant womb was created by the command of God in our text today. The creative power of Elohim released through the spoken word conditioned the earth turning it into a plant sprouting and sustaining machine, an incubation center for propagating life, efforts, and deeds.

People over the ages have tapped into this power of the earth to create better lives for themselves and others. They invested dreams, visions, and diligent labor to harvest

ORDER FROM CHAOS

gardens of delight that have fed and blessed nations in various domains. We live in the world they farmed. Think of Jesus, the corn of wheat that fell to the ground and died, now bringing forth much fruit.

Can you see this miraculous production system all around you? Planet earth is still pulsating with reproductive power to take what you plant in it, grow, and return it to you in multiplied form. The earth is waiting to sprout your seed, grow your crops and produce fruit-bearing trees for you in any domain you engage it with diligence. Deposit seed in the giant womb. Start farming.

"Plant your seed in the morning and keep busy all afternoon, for you don't know if profit will come from one activity or another—or maybe both (Ecc 11:6 NLT).

Decision of the Day

I understand that the earth is a giant womb, empowered to reproduce by the command of God. This command for the earth to sprout vegetation goes beyond just plants and covers all life domains. This system is designed to reward the diligent and faithful sower of seeds. I choose to be one today. I will engage it through diligence in my work and goodness in my deeds.

| DAY 11

THE HIDDEN FUTURE IN NOW

"The earth brought forth vegetation, plants yielding seed according to their own kinds, and trees bearing fruit in which is their seed, each according to its kind. And God saw that it was good."

— Genesis 1:12

A riddle:
I am Tomorrow in Today.
I was Today in Yesterday.
I was Now in Then
I am Then in Now.
Who am I?

I am Seed.

Today, we learn about another aspect of God's creative wisdom, the embedding of the future in the now. While the plants and trees brought forth from the earth at His command served an immediate purpose in the ecosystem, within them were also seeds that served a future purpose, ensuring their perpetuity. Both the present

ORDER FROM CHAOS

and the future were merged into one by our all-wise Creator.

This is another revelation of the way God works. He hides the future within Now. For example, an apple seed embedded in an apple is potentially another apple. Beyond that, it is potentially an orchard. Beyond that, it is several orchards—even a whole forest of apple trees—that would have more seeds that continue the sequence of reproduction exponentially. Thus, the original apple is given a life that extends beyond its own life and gets to continue living years after it has died.

This is a powerful principle in God's creation. Every living thing has its seed in it and can perpetuate itself.

People produce more people.
Love can perpetuate love.
Joy can perpetuate joy.
Generosity breeds more generosity.
Forgiveness can birth more forgiveness.
Mercy shown generates more mercy.

Even things you have in your life now can replicate.
Ideas can generate more ideas
Money can produce more money
Friendship nurtured can birth more friendships

Another powerful thing about seeds is the power of leverage that they possess. First, they leverage their sizes.

They don't have to be huge to fulfill their purpose. They are usually small in size compared to what they become when planted. They also leverage time by extending their current lives into the future.

This is good news! The little you may have don't have to be supersized to be viable. Just come as you are. Bring it as it is. Let the acorn fall to the ground to morph into the mighty oak tree.

A caution, though, the future of the seed is not an ironclad prophecy assured of fulfillment no matter what, but it exists as a possibility of potential. If it is eaten, its future perishes in the eater's belly. And though this is a tragedy, unfortunately, we often eat our tomorrow now. Hoarding, inability to delay gratification, a consumption mentality, and laziness are ways we eat the future now.

So today, decide to honor everything you have been given. Scrutinize your life and find where the future has been embedded. Bring it to the forefront and start investing it in the now.

Get on your knees and invest time in prayer.

Invest in wisdom as you read.

Train that voice and let it sing.

Fill that brain with knowledge. Force it to think creatively.

Build those strategic relationships one phone call at a time.

Buy the future now.

Today.

ORDER FROM CHAOS

Decision of the Day

I understand the power of a seed. It is the future embedded in now. It is small, but when planted, it can grow exponentially. It is here now, but it can potentially change the future. My life is loaded with seeds. I am pregnant with my future. I chose to begin investing my seeds. I decide to start buying the future now.

| DAY 12

A BRIEFER HISTORY OF TIME

"And God said, "Let there be lights in the expanse of the heavens to separate the day from the night. And let them be for signs and for seasons, and for days and years"

- Genesis 1:14

The Italian astronomer, and physicist Galileo, was persecuted by the Catholic Church because they believed he contradicted Scripture by championing the Copernican model of the universe in which the sun is at the center, and the earth and other planets revolve around it. As part of his defense, he made a significant statement: "The Scriptures were given, not to tell us how the heavens go, but to teach us how to go to heaven."

It is essential to note this when reading the Bible. We must not see it as a scientific book because it is not. It is a book that uses several human literature genres and everyday language to communicate answers to the higher questions of existence that God wants us to have. Its focus is not on scientific details. This is not to say that it does not provide scientifically sound answers and others that science eventually catches up with.

Today our focus is on the concept of time, one of the holy grails of physics. My goal is not to pull a Stephen Hawking here but to expound on some essential and practical inferences on time from the text.

Our text today was not time's first mention in Genesis. There was already an element of time in the first sentence, "In the beginning…" and in the subsequent references to evening, morning, and day. However, today's text was when time took center stage with reference to the measurement and marking of seasons, days, and years.

So here are a few things we can infer about time in Genesis 1:

1. Time had a beginning. Though it took science years to come to this conclusion, it is clear from the first word in Genesis, "In the beginning…". The earlier belief was that the universe was infinite.
2. God created time. Since He created time, He is superior to it, existed before it, and exists beyond it. He can control and manipulate time.
3. Time was one of the three aspects of nature (space (the heavens), time, and matter (earth)) immediately created in Genesis.
4. Time is one-dimensional but has three divisions of perception: past, present, and future. While

humans are bound to the present and can only remember the past and dream of the future, God is beyond time and can see both the past, present, and future as one eternal now (Isaiah 46:9-10).
5. For humans, time is perceived to be moving in a forward direction (evening to morning to evening to morning). This goes on and on.
6. Time is finite and measurable. Some of the measures mentioned in Genesis 1 include days, months, and years. Time allows us to track cycles of recurrences and festivities. The word used for this in our text today is "seasons."
7. The importance of the proper utilization and tracking of time is implied in our text today. The solar bodies were put there to help us do this.

So, what do all these mean to you? First, it should be a delight to know that several of these revelations of time in Genesis took millennials of research and millions of dollars expended for science to come to similar conclusions as the Bible.

Then, it is essential to think deeper about this commodity of time because it is the measure of your physical existence and the unit of your life. Time is the non-renewable raw material you convert to other things in your life. Understanding that it is a gift from the Creator that should be treasured, honored, and stewarded to fulfill His purpose for your earthly existence.

Finally, you should be encouraged that your creator lives outside of time, created time, and controls time. It means your past, present, and future are secure in Him. Since He controls it, He can intervene on your behalf when called upon to help you straighten out the wrinkles in time you will undoubtedly face in your sojourn on the earth.

Decision of the Day

I am so glad about the revelation of time: its creation, beginning, nature, and purpose. I am grateful for the opportunity to be in time right now to fulfill God's purpose. My time is in God's hands, and I have decided today to be a great steward of this gift, to convert it into beautiful experiences, and always remember that it is finite and must be maximized.

| DAY 13

VARIETY IS THE SPICE

"And God said, "Let the earth bring forth living creatures according to their kinds—livestock and creeping things and beasts of the earth according to their kinds." And it was so. ²⁵ And God made the beasts of the earth according to their kinds and the livestock according to their kinds, and everything that creeps on the ground according to its kind. And God saw that it was good."

- Genesis 1:24,25

Australian Shepherds, Dalmatians, Bulldogs, Chowchows, Poodles, Beagles, and Labradors. These are all examples of dog breeds that humans keep as household pets. There are also other non-domesticated or wild dogs like wolves and coyotes. These wild or domesticated dogs can interbreed, and the result would still be a dog kind. All is well and good.

However, if you take any of these dog breeds and try to mate them with, say a horse breed, then there is a problem. You have moved from one kind to another.

ORDER FROM CHAOS

So, there is a humankind (or mankind), a chicken kind, a horse kind, a cat kind, and so on. Kinds also exist in the plant world.

I hope you get my drift. I couldn't think of a better way to explain the word "kind" used in our text for today.

You will notice that there are a variety of combinations that can exist within a kind as interbreeding occurs. Also, environmental influences and genetic interactions can increase these differences within the kinds.

This is called Variation in biology. This explains why we have, for example, humans with freckles, dimples, different hair colors, different skin colors, varying heights, different blood types, and so on.

Our text today informs us that variation was the intent of the Creator from the very beginning. While there are delineations between kinds, such as cat and dog kind (they don't mix), or humans and bulls (sorry minotaur fans), the possible variations within kinds are not fixed.

If this biodiversity serves as a clue, our Creator must be a lover of variety. Obviously! The last part of our text today tells us He saw it was good. Diversity is great! The creator endorsed it. But why?

If you ask a biologist, their first answer would likely be "survival" —the so-called survival of the fittest. Differences mean responses to adverse conditions would be different. For example, a better runner can outrun a tiger while a snail-pace runner becomes lunch. I think there is a level of truth to this, but not in how the evolutionists see it.

ORDER FROM CHAOS

I see it more like something we were taught in engineering—redundancy, and reliability. Simply said, it would be "the more, the merrier" or "don't put all your eggs in one basket." Two engines in an airplane are better than one. Having two eyes, two ears, two lungs, and two kidneys is better than having one. It adds stability to the system. One goes, and the other continues the work.

I believe one of the reasons why God created a biodiverse world is for the continuity of his plan for the earth. You can stop one, but you can't stop all. I try to say this to people complaining about the proliferation of churches with all kinds of names, visions, worship styles, and banners. The more, the merrier. If the mega church is attacked, the home church continues because it can be more clandestine. If the tiny home church is facing difficulty, the big church can step in with resources and influence.

Also, it will take all kinds of churches to reach all types of people and advance the church's mission. So, in these ways, variation strengthens God's plan and makes it more resilient to malevolent forces.

Another benefit of diversity is the better expression of God's beauty. If God is infinite, as shown in Genesis, and if creation is to reflect his image, creation cannot be monotonous or homogeneous; it must be diverse and multifaceted. It will take this multivarious expression of God to fully express His manifold wisdom in a beautiful tapestry of all shapes and colors. By the way, God is not color blind. He created color.

Finally, diversity makes available various strengths, skills, perspectives, and approaches that can come together that give a better chance for the purposes of God on the earth to be fulfilled.

This is also why the church is typified as a body with many members and one of the reasons for the failed endeavor to build a tower to reach heaven (I'm getting ahead of myself. We will read about this later) and situate everyone in one location with one language. God's plan was spread. Their own was constriction. God's way won.

So, embrace diversity in your life. Find your kind, your company, your lane. That's ok. But don't build a silo. Reach out to those unlike you. Learn from them. Collaborate with them. It's going to take all kinds.

Decision of the Day

I understand that the diversity in creation is God's original intent. It makes us stronger and helps us better reflect on the excellent glory of God. I will embrace it and make it a part of my approach to life.

| DAY 14

PRIMARY PURPOSE

"And God said, let us make human beings in our own image, to be like us..."

- Genesis 1:26

The purpose of a thing dictates its design. Understanding man's design gives us a glimpse into his purpose. Humanity was made in the image and likeness of God. We know this is not referring to man's physical body since God is Spirit with no physical body (John 4:24), so it must be referring to another part of man, his spiritual and soul nature.

What are some of the aspects of the image of God in humanity?

1. Speech: humans are the only talking beings among all of God's creation. They can communicate with language.

2. Intelligence and Creativity: of all of God's creation, humans are the only ones who can think original thoughts and turn those thoughts into new innovative designs.

3. **Freedom:** humans are the only ones in God's creation with the capacity for choice. They are even free to reject God.

4. **Love:** humans are the only ones in God's creation with the capacity to love Him and have a relationship with Him. That is why even though your dog has some capacity for emotions, it will never seek God. It will never have a desire for God, and even though it sees you praying or worshipping, it has no understanding of such higher love.

5. **Righteousness and Holiness.** Mankind, in his original state, was pure and holy. The remnant of that trait is still seen in fallen man. He craves beauty and excellence.

6. **Immortality:** even though man's body became subject to death because of sin, his spirit is immortal and will live forever either with God or in eternal separation from Him.

This is not an exhaustive list of the manifestation of the image of God in mankind, but these should be enough to convince you that you are created to live a higher kind of life and that there is a unique purpose for you in God's design. There is a reason why God created you in His class of being, a little lower than Elohim, according to Psalm 8:5.

He created you primarily because He wanted a family, which He could shower His love on.

Love always seeks the opportunity for expression through giving. He wanted people in His image and likeness who would be capable of fellowship with Him. True fellowship requires beings of the same order. You could be friends with your cat, but you could never enjoy true intimacy with it. You need another human to enjoy intimacy. In the same way, God desiring fellowship made man in His image and likeness with the capacity to love and communicate with Him intelligently.

This is the reason why humans have an insatiable craving for intimacy. The famous mathematician and philosopher Blaise Pascal said it this way:

"What else does this craving, and this helplessness, proclaim but that there was once in man a true happiness, of which all that now remains is the empty print and trace? This he tries in vain to fill with everything around him, seeking in things that are not there the help he cannot find in those that are, though none can help, since this infinite abyss can be filled only with an infinite and immutable object; in other words, by God Himself."

In other words, there is a God-shaped hole in every man's heart that only God can fill.

Would you decide today to make seeking this primary purpose your priority in life? Would you make knowing and developing intimacy with this loving God your chief aim? Would you draw near to Him today in worship and prayer and make it your daily quest to know Him? This is the path to meeting your deepest longings and to true fulfillment in life.

Decision of the Day

I understand that I am made in the image and likeness of God because God wants a relationship with me. I now know that my craving for intimacy can never be satisfied by man or things. Only God can fill the void in my heart and bring true fulfillment. My primary purpose is to know Him intimately. From today I will draw near to Him. I will acknowledge and pursue my desire for Him. I will make time spent in worship, prayer, and reading His word a priority in my life.

| DAY 15

SECONDARY PURPOSE

"And God said, let us make man in our own image and after our likeness and let them have dominion..."

- Genesis 1:26

As there are two sides to a coin, but it is the same coin, and so is the purpose of God for humanity. There is the primary purpose which is intimacy with God through fellowship. There is also a secondary purpose revealed in this verse.

As the created man found his place in fellowship with God, through the influence of God on him, he was commanded and equipped to exercise dominion on the earth. He was made to be God's delegated ruler. His purpose was to extend God's rule and establish His will on the earth. He was to extend the kingdom of God in the earthly realm until the whole earth was filled with the glory of the Lord. He was to bring everything under subjection to the will of God.

ORDER FROM CHAOS

Since God's purposes are unchangeable, this is still His purpose for humanity. We are to exercise dominion over the earth and utilize all its abundant resources to establish the will of God here. The ability to do this was greatly hindered by the fall of man, through which the control of the earth system was handed over by Adam to Satan (Luke 4:5), thus crowning him as the god of this world (2 Corinthians 4:4).

However, through the coming of the Lord Jesus and His victory over Satan in His death and resurrection, all authority in heaven and on earth is now given back to those who put their trust in His sacrifice and make Him their Lord (Matt 28:18-20). In His name, we have the authority restored back to us to exercise dominion over the earth.

If you have made Jesus your Lord, you have that authority now in His name. You have the authority to pray in the Name of Jesus and see mighty things happen in the earthly realm. You have the authority to rebuke and resist Satan in your submission to God and he will flee from you (James 4:7).

God has deputized you to enforce His will revealed in His word in your sphere of life. Your sphere includes your body and mind, your home, your place of work, or your place of assignment in your calling from God. Christ has commissioned you to go into your world and preach the gospel to everyone there with signs and wonders accompanying you.

So, what are you going to do with your dominion from today? Your exercise of it is an assignment handed over to you by God. First, you must reclaim your blood-bought freedom in Christ from everything that wants to hold you bound and hinder you from fulfilling your purpose: sin, sickness, oppression, lack of resources, insecurities, and fear. You were bought with a price, and these should not have dominion over you.

Second, there is a sphere of life where God has placed you, where He wants His will and way established through your life and your witness. You are God's kingdom carrier in that sphere. It could be in the arts and entertainment, business, church, media, educational, family, or government spheres.

Wherever it is, He wants you to exercise your dominion over that sphere until people around you come to Christ and the systems there start to conform to God's will and bring Him glory as they were intended to. This is your secondary purpose in life, a privilege God has given you. Use it.

Decision of the Day

I understand that my secondary purpose is to bring God's rule into the sphere of life in which God has placed me. I have been given authority to reclaim my total freedom from Satan and his works through His name. It is not God's will for me to bow to Satan's whims, but I am to resist him. I am also to be a witness for Christ where I live and work. I will lead people to submit to Christ's Lordship through my lifestyle, prayer, and sharing. Today, in the name of Jesus, I declare that I am free and rebuke Satan and all his works in my life. I also will begin to witness to people in my sphere about Christ and His work of salvation.

| DAY 16

BE FRUITFUL AND MULTIPLY

"Then God blessed them and said, "Be fruitful and multiply. Fill the earth and govern it. Reign over the fish in the sea, the birds in the sky, and all the animals that scurry along the ground."

- Genesis 1:28

Be fruitful and multiply. This statement is repeated up to six times in the book of Genesis. It is God's way of ensuring the perpetuity of His works and the proliferation of it all over the earth.

First, it shows us the goal of God for the earth, that there should be an exponential multiplication of everything that He created all over the earth until the earth was teeming with them. It shows us that God is abundance-minded. Scarcity, decrease, lack of growth, or barrenness wasn't in His original plan for the earth.

Then we see that He released something from Himself that would foster this purpose of multiplication – the blessing. The blessing was released as a result of God's command, and it is a force that works upon creation to

ORDER FROM CHAOS

cause it to tend toward constant and never-ending increase. This force is talked about more in the subsequent chapters of Genesis.

God and His purpose have not changed. The command to be fruitful and multiply and the blessing that comes with it to accomplish it, is still on you. Believer, it is against the order of God for things to keep shrinking. The order of God is increase and expansion.

Look at your life now and inventory everything God has blessed you with your physical life, intelligence, information, talents, gifts, finances, career, influence, opportunities, children, faith, love, testimony, and so on. Understand that God's purpose for everything you have now is that they tend toward increase. Whenever things begin to shrink or remain stagnant, another force is in operation contrary to the blessing. The blessing of God produces an increase.

What do you do if you find that your life is stagnant, that you are no longer multiplying and bringing more people to Christ, that your life seems to be contained by some forces in a never-ending circle of scarcity, that your business, ministry, or opportunities seem to be shrinking? First, confront the situation by acknowledging that this is against God's divine order. Christ said, "Herein is my Father glorified, that you bear much fruit..." (John 15:8). Don't rationalize. Refuse the religious thinking that you glorify God by constantly living in scarcity and containment. God has a purpose for your life that requires you to expand your coast continuously until more and more of His investment in your life influences more people. He has increase on His mind for you.

Then, check your connection to God's blessing, which is evident in the quality of your fellowship with Him and your obedience to His word. God's word is the blessing source (Psalm 1:1-3). Are you saturating your life with it and letting it dictate your walk and decisions? Find out what He has said about that area of life where you feel contained and begin to practice and speak what you see in His word. Soon that great force of increase and multiplication will break every containment and make your life more fruitful for His glory.

Decision of the Day

I understand that increase and multiplication are God's intention for my life, not scarcity and containment. Everything in my life that He has given me should grow and exert more influence for Him on the earth. I also see that the blessing of God is the root of increase and multiplication. This blessing increases on me as I honor His word, practice it, and fellowship with it. I will saturate my life with His word, hearing, speaking, singing, and obeying it. I will abide in the Vine and let His word abide in me, and every force of containment will be broken off my life so that I can be more fruitful for His glory.

| DAY 17

SEED CONSCIOUSNESS

"Then God blessed them and said, "Be fruitful and multiply. Fill the earth and govern it. Reign over the fish in the sea, the birds in the sky, and all the animals that scurry along the ground."

- Genesis 1:28

We looked at this verse yesterday, but we are not done with it. There are still more gems hidden in it. So, we will still examine it today. The best thing that can happen to an apple seed is not that it is eaten or thrown away but that it is planted. If planted, then it has a chance to produce an apple tree that produces more apples. It is said to be fruitful if it goes through that process of being planted and begins to yield more apples. Fruitfulness is the ability of a thing to reproduce itself.

God blessed and commanded them to be fruitful. In other words, God empowered them to reproduce themselves. God was saying, in essence, that He had invested His dream for the earth, which is to see it filled and subdued, but that dream was placed in them as seeds that must be planted before it became a reality. Adam and Eve were walking houses of God's dream. Billions of humans were in them in potential seed form. They were to get involved in the reproductive process of planting these seeds, replicating themselves over and over.

It is important to note that this was not restricted to Adam and Eve. God did the same thing for everything He created. They were all given the ability to reproduce after their kinds. The blessing would work if they planted the seed.

You are not exempted from this law. You, too, are a walking house of the seeds of God's dream for a part of the earth. You are a seed planted by God on the planet. Everything you are that is in you or your life now is a seed.

Your physical life, thoughts, word, talents, experience, love, strength, habits, possessions, relationships, knowledge, and other things in your life are now seeds. Everything you will ever be is already in your life in potential form. God never needs to do anything new for humans, animals, or plants to reproduce. All they must do is engage in His established process. In the same way, you only need to get into His process of planting and replicate.

The blessing of God will work if you plant these seeds in your life. To maximize the blessing of God that was released, you must become seed minded. Plant knowledge by sharing it. Plant your faith by sharing it. Plant your finances by investing them in loving God and others. Plant your dreams by diligently working on them—plant good thoughts and words in your life.

Plant good habits. Remember, everything is blessed to be fruitful. Don't be intimidated by how little things look in your life now. Think like a farmer. The process works indiscriminately. Even bad seeds are blessed to reproduce. Whatever a man sows, he will reap. Never forget. Your future is already in your life now, waiting to be planted.

Decision of the Day

I understand that I am a walking house of seeds, and that God has blessed those seeds to reproduce. My future is with me now. I need to get involved in the process of planting, and God's dreams for me will emerge. Everything in my life can increase as I plant them. Today, I will become a sower. I will start thinking like a farmer, sowing my life, and watching the blessing of God increase my influence for Him.

| DAY 18

PREMIUM FOOD

"And God said, "Behold, I have given you every plant yielding seed that is on the face of all the earth, and every tree with seed in its fruit. You shall have them for food"

- Genesis 1:29

Ever since we were in our 30s, my wife, Debo, and I became more aware of the effect of our lifestyle, especially our diet, on our health. So, we started scrutinizing our diet. The first to go was processed sugar. That was simple enough. We made a few other changes. But then followed the confusion.

We watched and read from various diet gurus, doctors, and nutritionists, some often contradicting one another. "Go Keto," "Eat Mediterranean," "The Zone, Diet is the bomb," "Go Vegan," "Try Vegetarian," "Paleo is the newest thing now," "Try the Ornish, Hypercaloric, Volumetric, Hypocaloric Diets… See how confusing it can all be.

After a while, we had to tune out all the din and settle on what worked for us. I found a few passages in the Bible

ORDER FROM CHAOS

that spoke to diets and decided that we would make these the basis of our diet choices. At the same time, we continue to be thankful, bless our food, and trust God that if we ate any deadly thing inadvertently, it would not hurt us (1 Timothy 4:4, Mark 16:18). Our text today is one of those passages of Scripture.

The first striking thing about this passage is how the care of God for humanity. The issue of our feeding is not too menial for him to get involved in. He cares enough to provide for us and to guide us in our choices. It reminds me of when Jesus said we should not worry about what we shall eat or drink because our heavenly father knows our needs and has made provision for us in His kingdom (Matt 6:25-27)

Also, every responsible manufacturer includes a maintenance guide with their products. Car manufacturers usually specify the minimum octane grade of gasoline required for the proper functioning of the car. The creator is a manufacturer too, so it is no surprise that He would recommend a diet for His prized creation. Let's dig into the recommendation.

Later in the Bible, there will be other recommendations, but our focus, for now, is this passage. There are two types of food mentioned here.

Every plant yielding seed
Every tree with seed in its fruit

The first conclusion here is that the premium food initially recommended for the optimum performance of humanity was plant-based, and it wouldn't be too much of a jump to say that this should constitute most of our diet even now.

This should be the foundation of our diet plan. God did not recommend eating animals here though He would do that later after the flood. It is also interesting to know that when Israel was in the wilderness for 40 years, God's preference of food for them was manna, which was not animal-based. Only when Israel began to crave meat did God send the quails to their camp. I am not saying meat is wrong or should be excluded but that the foundation of our diet should be plant-based.

Even when he allowed them to eat animals, there were strict instructions on the type of animal, the state of the animal when it died, and the prohibition from eating its blood.

The plant-based food recommended had the following characteristics:

1. They were simple, natural, and easily digestible food
2. They included seeds and fruits, which were nature's ready-made food that required little or no cooking
3. They were separate from what was recommended for the animals.

4. They looked good and were delicious to the taste (Gen 2:9).

From these characteristics, I extracted the following guideline for the food I would choose. Join me in making this your decision today, too, if it works for you.

Decision of the Day

1. Most of my meals will be plant-based food.
2. I will look for the most natural form of these plants, eating organic whenever available. I will even plant mine when I can.
3. I will avoid genetically modified fruits as much as I can, going for fruits with seeds.
4. I will eat more living foods that require little or no cooking.
5. The simpler the food, the better. I will avoid highly processed, stimulating, and complex food.
6. I will eat food that is pleasant to look at and delicious to taste. This would require me to retrain my taste buds to enjoy simple food.
7. I will eat in consideration of my activity level and fast food regularly so my body can cleanse itself. When I am involved in work that expends physical energy, I eat a different type of food than when I am sedentary or using brain power.

| DAY 19

GOD IS GOOD

"And God saw everything that he had made and behold [it was] very good. And the evening and the morning were the sixth day."

- Genesis 1:31

It is sometimes hard for religious minds to comprehend a benevolent God who was excited about doing good to His creatures at every opportunity.

The late evangelist Oral Roberts used to ruffle many feathers when he made statements like, "something good is going to happen to you," "expect a miracle," or "God is a good God." Many religious people would get mad at those statements.

The statement seemed off because of the past emphasis in the religious world on Calvinistic doctrines of human depravity and a judgmental God.

Of course, the Calvinist God was (and is) technically good, too, but Oral Roberts seemed to emphasize that He was only good and extra good. There shouldn't have been any uproar about the statement because it is very consistent with the revelation of God throughout the bible.

From today's verse up to the New Testament, many portions of scripture give us a glimpse of the goodness of God. In the creation account alone, there are at least 14 times when God judged the success of His creation by the fact that it was good. In a particular instant, He discovered something that was not good, the man being alone, and immediately went to work fixing it, creating Eve.

It shows us that God assessed Himself by the goodness of His works. In other parts of the scriptures, He is shown as abundant in goodness (Exodus 34:6), having great goodness (Psalm 31:19), one who should be praised for his goodness (Psalm 107:8), the good father who gives only good gifts to His children (Matthew 7:11), having goodwill toward men (Luke 2:14) and the source of all good things who does not change as shifting shadows (James 1:17).

The opposite of good is evil, and both the Old and New Testaments emphasize that God has no evil or darkness. He is all good. We are told to "give thanks to the LORD, for he is good! His faithful love endures forever" (Psalm 136:1). When Jesus, who is the perfect manifestation of the Father, came, it was said of Him, "How God anointed Jesus of Nazareth with the Holy Ghost and with power: who went about doing good and healing all that were oppressed of the devil; for God was with him" (Acts 10:38).

God is good. The gospel is glad tidings of good things (How beautiful are the feet of them that preach the gospel of peace and bring glad tidings of good things! (Romans 10:15)). God has no evil in Him. His thoughts for you are thoughts of good. He is the very personification of goodness. He is always thinking of how to do you good and work every situation in your life for good.

He is not a malevolent God who sends earthquakes and disasters as the insurance companies accuse Him of doing. He is not the author of sickness and pain as some religious people accuse Him of being. He has no incentive to cause cancer or a car accident to teach you a lesson.

A lesson or good may come from such incidents, but that is not God's original plan. He plans to teach you through His word and by His Spirit. You wouldn't break your child's leg or pray for Him to have cancer to teach Him a lesson. How much more God, the source of all fatherhood - the most incredible Father?

Today, begin to believe in the goodness of God. Let His goodness floods your mind right now until He changes that caricature of Him that religion may have taught you. Expect His goodness today. Sing the song of Israel. Give Him thanks, for He is good, and His mercy endures forever. Even if you are in a situation that looks like everything is contrary to goodness: maybe you just lost a loved one, or you are sick of a terminal disease, or you just failed at a business, or you are going through a divorce, give Him thanks and let His goodness work things out for your good. Today, expect a miracle! Something good is about to happen to you because God is good all the time!

Decision of the Day

I understand that the revelation of God in the bible is that He is good. Perfectly good and only good. His thoughts towards me are good. He loves to shower my life with good things. All good things proceed from Him. Jesus personified Him on earth by His goodness. He did no evil but went about healing and helping all. Healing is good. His words are good. Today, I boldly declare that something good is going to happen to me. I am expecting God's best. I am thankful to God for He is good, and His love endures forever toward me.

| DAY 20

HOLY TIME

"By the seventh day God had finished the work he had been doing; so on the seventh day he rested from all his work. Then God blessed the seventh day and made it holy, because on it he rested from all the work of creating that he had done."

- Genesis 2:2-3

Many writings about the Sabbath debate questions such as, "Which day is the Sabbath?" and "How did the Sabbath day become Sunday?" That is not our intention here. Our purpose is to understand the principle of the Sabbath and its purpose. We know God never does anything without a purpose, so there must be one for this initiative of God.

In our verse today, God, having completed the extensive work of creation, shifts into a new mode of fellowship and training. He took off work and rested on the seventh day. Then He sanctified the day as holy Jesus clarified the purpose for us, saying, "The Sabbath was made for man and not man for the Sabbath." (Mark 2:27). So, the Sabbath was an initiative with the benefit of man in mind, not a legalistic requirement that keeps man in bondage to a day.

The concept of the Sabbath is a "holy time" during which man can fellowship with God, be refreshed, and receive fresh wisdom and impetus for the work that lies ahead of taking God's creation to its maximum potential. In other words, after God finished His part in the work of creation, He handed the baton to man to take it to the next level.

Humankind was to subdue creation, tend it, discover its hidden potential, and use it maximally to show the beauty of God on the earth. He was to make earth the garden spot and the most desirable place in the universe.

To do this, however, man must have a holy time of rest and refreshing, when God can coach the man in reigning when God's wisdom can distill into mankind. In this place of fellowship, man would learn about the beautiful works of God and the purpose of each and then go forth to combine pieces of creation and bring forth secondary masterpieces.

In this holy time of rest and communion, Man was to receive inspiration for witty inventions, poetry and wordsmith abilities, artistic forms, music, and all the various creative expressions we see now. The Sabbath time would be a time of learning and inspiration that would provide the impetus for creativity and dominion. Man would fan into greater flame the glory of God on him, take it, and cover the earth with it.

The Sabbath was to be a meeting of kings, the King of the universe and His subordinate king of the earth. It was to be the council of emperors, a gathering of lords, and a fellowship and business meeting of Father and Sons Incorporated. The first one took place on the first full day of man, the seventh day (remember, he was created on the sixth day). This shows the priority. Adam must have opened His eyes to see God in a restful mode in the cool of the day. He started his time with rest and with God.

So, what is the significance of this to you? The principle of the Sabbath still holds. Holy time is still required for you to function maximally on the earth. Suppose your endeavors in ministry, relationships, career, or otherwise must achieve their highest potential. In that case, a priority portion of your time must be spent with God in rest and fellowship. This is no longer attached to a particular day or time but a personally chosen time when you can shut up yourself with God in prayer, worship, and reading or hearing His word.

It could be some minutes or hours each day, a day, or some days each week or month where you turn your full attention to God and let His power, wisdom, peace, and grace engulf your life until your whole being enters into His rest of faith. His person will rub off on you, and you will begin to take on His attributes.

People will perceive that you have been with Him as your weaknesses begin to dissolve under His influence and His influence on you starts to make you influential for Him on the earth. This is an adventure you must commence today. Remember, the Sabbath was made for you.

Decision of the Day

I understand that the Sabbath was made to benefit me. God initiated the principle of "holy time" so that, as a priority, He will be able to spend time in fellowship with me and impart His grace and wisdom on me for victory during my work time. It is a time of rejuvenation, refreshing, and rest for me. It is when I meet with God and have Him teach, inspire, and direct me. My work must start with rest and peace to be creative. I decide today to prioritize "holy time" in my life. I will apportion specific blocks of time to be with God and fellowship with Him.

| DAY 21

NATURAL HABITAT

"The Lord God took the man and put him in the Garden of Eden to work it and take care of it."

- Genesis 2:15

In the first part of our text today, God took the man and put him in the Garden of Eden. This is first a reference to man's environment. God's first thing after He made man was to plant him in an environment optimal for fulfilling his purpose and maximized living.

The newly created Adam was humanity in its perfect state. God's following steps regarding Adam reveal to us God's original plan for humans and the fundamental essence of maximized humanity as God intended it.

That environment was the Garden of Eden. What was the atmosphere of Eden? Primarily, it was an atmosphere saturated with the presence of God. It was a spot on the earth where God would come to fellowship with man. It was unique and separated from the rest of the earth because God visited His man there. It was a meeting place between

God and man, a tabernacle where God's presence intercepted the earth. We see this implied in Genesis 4:16, "So Cain left the LORD's presence and settled in the land of Nod, east of Eden." After the fall, the presence of God was in Eden, guarded by angels, with man expelled, longing to go back but settling in regions all around it.

So initially, humanity was created to live in an atmosphere saturated by the presence of God. The word Eden means delight. Psalm 16:11 says, "in His presence is fulness of joy and at his right hand are pleasures evermore." Eden was a climate of joy and ecstasy, where man enjoyed fellowship with God and God with man.

To fully maximize your life, you must live in the atmosphere of God's presence. That is your natural habitat. When you became born again, the presence of God became available to you. He lives in you now. You must cultivate that presence in prayer, worship, and fellowship with Him until it becomes a manifested reality in your life.

Living outside God's presence is like being a fish out of water. Without the manifested presence of God, the real you, your spirit, begins to die. Your flesh begins to rule over you, and eventually, your whole being, spirit, soul, and body will start showing symptoms of being cut off from your spiritual source. This is the reason for the lack of joy, irritability, complaint, worry, powerlessness, strife, and lovelessness displayed by many of us sometimes.

Whenever you start seeing any of such symptoms in your life, check your devotional life. Are you still consistent in prayer? Is it still your priority to fill yourself with God's word by reading and meditating on it? Are you still spending time in worship and fellowship with God and with fellow believers? Is there any unconfessed sin in your life?

Satan will do whatever He can to trick you out of God's presence, for then he can afflict you with woes as he chooses. If you know you are out of it, decide today to get back in God's presence and live there. Say like the Psalmist, "Surely goodness and mercy shall follow me all the days of my life, and I will dwell in the house (presence) of the Lord forever and ever" (Psalm 23:6).

Decision of the Day

I understand that the presence of God is the atmosphere I was created to live in. Just as God put Adam in Eden, He has made His company available to me by putting me in Christ and letting Christ live in me through the Holy Spirit. I must cultivate that presence by being aware of it and fellowshipping with God. It is my decision today that I will not live without His presence again. I will seek and love Him, acknowledging His presence in my life. I will not grieve Him by my lifestyle but will live in reverence of Him. Living is not I alone again, but my Lord and I.

| DAY 22

A REVELATION OF WORK

"The Lord God took the man and put him in the Garden of Eden to work it and take care of it."

- Genesis 2:15

The principle of working and compensation is ingrained in nature. Someone has remarked that even though God gives birds food, He doesn't throw it into their nests. Ants are famous for their diligence in storing food up for the wintertime.

As we continue our meditation on the essence of maximized humanity as intended by God, we see that the next thing God did after placing man in His Garden was to inform him of His essential responsibilities. He gave him an assignment. His work was to take care of the garden. We can learn a few things from this regarding Adam's work that can teach us more about God's design for our work.

1. Work as Worship: Adam's work was an assignment from God, and so it was part of His obedience and thus worship to God. Work is divinely delegated. It is not just a job. It is a divine assignment. Your work is worship too.

2. Work as Preordained: Adam did not have to choose his work. His work was selected for Him before He arrived by God. It was only made known to him at this time. Your real work and assignment in life were preordained, too (Ephesians 2:10).

3. Work Discovery Preceding Wife Discovery: Adam was given his assignment before he was given a wife. His wife was to be a helper in his God-given mission. Discover your work, and spouse discovery will follow naturally.

4. Work as Partnership with God: Good Work involves the tending, caring, and tilling of God's creation. It is focused on improving, loving, spreading, tapping into the potential, or preserving some aspects of God's creation. It is maintaining the work God Himself began, tending the garden God planted. You are a co-laborer with God, too (1 Corinthians 3:9).

5. Work as Problem Solving: Work is meeting a need and solving a problem. Creation needed a ruler; the garden required a keeper. Adam's work was to solve this problem. You are created to solve a particular problem too.

6. Work as Fitting Natural Endowments: Adam was naturally endowed for his work. He had the intelligence, dominion, and inherent tools to carry out His assignment. You are also uniquely designed for your assignment.

7. Work will be Compensated: "And the Lord God commanded the man, "You are free to eat from any tree in the garden..." (Genesis 2:16). From the beginning, God established the principle of compensation that those who work should eat from their work. This principle is reiterated in the law, and the New Testament (Deuteronomy 25:4, I Timothy 5:18, 1 Corinthians 9:9). Conversely, those who don't work should not eat (2 Thessalonians 3:10). Don't look to man for your compensation. Work hard, expecting God to compensate you!

8. The Tithe of Work: "...but you must not eat from the tree of the knowledge of good and evil, for when you eat from it you will certainly die." Genesis 2:17. Adam was to till the whole garden. A part of his work result will be the blooming and fruitfulness of this tree, but he was not to eat the fruit. A portion of the product of his work was holy and separated to the Lord and must not be consumed by him. This is the tithe principle of considering a part of the fruit of your work consecrated to the Lord. Obey this principle by always separating a part of your income as dedicated to God's use.

9. Work as Blessedly Sweet Not Stressful Sweats: "To Adam, he said, "Because you listened to your wife and ate fruit from the tree about which I commanded you, 'You must not eat from it,' "Cursed is the ground because of you; through painful toil, you will eat food from it all the days of your life. It will produce thorns and thistles for you, and you will eat the plants of the field. By the sweat of your brow, you will eat your food until you return to the ground..." (Genesis 3:17-19).

Adam was meant to work, not to toil painfully. Work was meant to be enjoyable and sweet. When you are doing the work you were created for, there will be a pleasure that comes with it.

10. Work Should Be Blessed: After the fall, work became a toil of sweat because of the curse. It is the blessing that multiplies labor to produce results. God promised to bless the works of our hands (Deuteronomy 28:12). The blessing has been restored to you in Christ. Laboring in the grace of the blessing will cause your work to be exceedingly fruitful.

Decision of the Day

I understand that my work is an assignment from God, so it is a part of my worship of Him. It is a blessed, preordained partnership with God to solve a problem and care for God's creation using the gifts and resources He has put in me. I am to enjoy my work both in doing and in compensation, giving a part of my compensation as worship to God. This I decide to do from today.

| DAY 23

POWER TO CHOOSE

"God commanded the Man, "You can eat from any tree in the garden, except from the Tree-of-Knowledge-of-Good-and-Evil. Don't eat from it. The moment you eat from that tree, you're dead."

- Genesis 2:16-17 MSG

If I was to rate the things we should be most grateful for, today's thought would be one of the top ones.
In our meditation on maximized humanity as God intended, we have identified two characteristics so far: living in God's presence and working at fulfilling a divine assignment. Today we look at another one, the ability to choose.

"You can eat from any tree in the garden" implies various choices. There was a wide variety of trees in the garden. "Any" means that Adam had the right to choose what he wanted from all the available options, meaning that God endowed Him with the power of choice. It was not only in this area that freedom to choose was given to him but in every area. He had the right to choose whatever he wanted for himself. He even had the right to choose to love God or not, or to obey Him or not. In other words, man, made in the image of God, is the chief determinant of his destiny. He is responsible for his life. He is a free moral agent. He is not a robot who will do or say what God wants as programmed. He is free to decide his actions after weighing the consequences. Only man was given this privilege out of all God's creatures.

You should be thankful to God for this gift. You have the power to choose. You are free. You are free to choose whom you serve, your location, friends, vocation, habit, emotion, words, and future. You are free to choose your eternal destiny, either in heaven or hell.

God will not impose on your will. You are ultimately responsible for your life. No one can take this privilege from you except you willfully surrender it through ignorance or fear or as the consequence of foolish actions such as crime when some of your choices become the state's responsibility.

Even if you are incarcerated, or on death row, you still have the freedom to choose how you will live and your eternal destiny. This God-given freedom is why you will be the one to give account for your life to God on the Day of Judgment, not your friends, parents, spouse, government, or pastor.

You may not be able to choose how others act, but you can decide how you do. You can choose your reactions to people when they act in unpleasant ways. You can also choose your emotions. Your feelings are subject to your will. You don't have to be sad except if you choose to be. To rejoice is a choice.

You don't have to hate anyone. Love is a decision of the will, not an emotion. You can choose peace rather than strife. Your feelings will follow your choices. You can choose health rather than sickness, blessings rather than curses.

God says: "Today I have given you the choice between life and death, between blessings and curses. Now I call on heaven and earth to witness the choice you make. Oh, that you would choose life so that you and your descendants might live!" (Deuteronomy 30:19 NLT)

Satan has always tried to deceive us to lead us into making the wrong choices. This is what temptation is. It is a solicitation to do evil. Sometimes he lies to us that we have no choice in an issue. Jesus said in John 8:32, "…you will know the truth, and the truth will set you free".

This is the truth: you are not to surrender to Satan's harassment or people's opinions contrary to God. You have the right to choose. Get the correct information and make your choice. Don't hesitate or vacillate between opinions. Use your God-given freedom to make the best decisions that glorify God, bless others, and advance your purpose in Him.

Decision of the Day

I understand that I am a free moral agent. I have the God-given ability to choose. I always have a choice in every issue. I will not allow indecision or fear to hinder me. I will not be pressured to make wrong choices. I am free to choose my emotions and reactions to circumstances and people. I will exercise my ability today to make the right choices.

| DAY 24

LEARNING TO SAY NO

"God commanded the Man, "You can eat from any tree in the garden, except from the Tree-of-Knowledge-of-Good-and-Evil. Don't eat from it. The moment you eat from that tree, you're dead."

- Genesis 2:16-17 MSG

Boundaries are prevalent in our world. Take a walk around your neighborhood. Everywhere you look, you will see boundaries: fences, hedges, no trespassing signs, wrong-way signs, moats, security signs, tinted car windows, gates, locked doors, road dividers, and landmarks. Even the clothes people wear are some kind of boundary. The laws of the society, immigration procedures, and the protection and shielding of public officials are all boundaries.

While verse 16 in our text is a statement of choice, as we observed yesterday, verse 17 is one of restriction and consequences. It was the institution of a boundary. Adam was not to eat from a particular tree. This boundary did not remove his power of choice but violating it would have consequences.

A boundary is a limit, a separation, or a borderline. It represents the extent to which something is allowed to go. The message of a boundary is, "don't go beyond this." A boundary is also used to delineate areas of responsibility. You are responsible for mowing your lawn, not your neighbors, so there is a demarcation between your properties.

In our text, God established the principle of boundaries in preparing His maximized man for living. Though man has the legal right to free and unlimited choices, he does not have the moral right to utilize every option. Some of the options are off-limits. There are boundaries he should not cross; otherwise, he would face unpleasant consequences.

Boundaries keep the good in and the bad out. This responsibility comes with the power to choose - to respect proper boundaries. It is the ability to say "yes" and "no" as the situation demands. God put that forbidden tree there to test Adam's ability to say no to eating its fruit and yes to His command.

Most of us have no problem saying yes but saying no to the wrong thing is the challenge. That is why our lives are filled with many loads we weren't supposed to carry and many actions and situations that required a "no" from us that we said "yes" to.

ORDER FROM CHAOS

Think of individuals who just can't say no to the demands of others even though they are detrimental to them. They spend their days complying with the excessive demands of friends, families, bosses, and others, even though they take their lives off balance. They take on the consequences of the mistakes of others and the problems and responsibilities of others while allowing them to continue living irresponsible lives.

This is typical with parents who have irresponsible children. Rather than confront the situation with decisive action, ending their subsidizing of reckless living and setting boundaries, they avoid saying no. We are to care for others, but we are not to shield them from the consequences of their actions to our hurt. We hurt people more when we do not allow them to taste and thus understand the consequences of their actions, which could lead them to change.

A life without boundaries is a frustrating life. It is a life without control. It is like a city without protection or security. The good that should stay in such lives escapes, and the bad that should go out stays in, inviting more in. It is a life without standards, standing for nothing and falling for everything. The extreme of this is what the New Testament calls lasciviousness, a total lack of restraint or control (2 Corinthians 12:20-21).

Do you have the proper boundaries in your life? Have you established some no-go areas of life rooted in the commands of God? Do your choices of entertainment, food, sexual expression, spending, relationships, dressing, language, or speech have the proper limits? Have you been able to differentiate between what you can control and what you can't? Have you been able to separate the load you are meant to carry from burdens being thrust on you because of the failures of others? Are you subsidizing another person's failures out of an improper understanding of your responsibility to love and care for others? God wants you to have limits. There are fruits in life you must not partake of.

Today, examine your life and ask God to help you set the proper boundaries. Start applying the limits of His word to your life. Start developing relationships with people who love and set boundaries and be accountable to one another. Respect other people's boundaries. Begin practicing the ability to say no politely, starting from little things. You cannot be at every party. You cannot do every task. You can't be everyone's friend or confidant. You cannot give to everyone and every project. You can't satisfy every demand of people. You can't be everything to your family. You are not God.

Practice rejoicing and rewarding yourself when you feel bad for saying no. Always remember that there are many fruits you may partake of in life, but you've got to say no to some, no matter how alluring they may be or how pressuring it is to eat them. This is maximized living.

Decision of the Day

I understand that though I have the power of choice, this power comes with the responsibility to set and respect boundaries. Today I decide to live a life with standards and control. I will begin to say no in situations that demand no for an answer though I may feel bad about it. I will learn to say yes to what is right. I will not try to be God, taking on responsibilities that belong only to Him. I will encourage others to be responsible by letting them see the consequences of their actions. I will not subsidize irresponsibility.

| DAY 25
CONSEQUENCES

"And the Lord God commanded the man, "You are free to eat from any tree in the garden; but you must not eat from the tree of the knowledge of good and evil, for when you eat from it you will certainly die."

- Genesis 2:16-17 NIV

Thomas Huxley, the scientist, once said in one of his lectures that, "a man's worst difficulties begin when he is able to do as he likes". Why? Because with great power comes great responsibility.

We are not done with these verses yet. So far, from them, we have meditated on the power of choice and the necessity of boundaries in life. Today we will look at another thing revealed in verse 17 – the truth about consequences.

"Consequence" is something that happens because of a previous action or condition. It logically follows and depends on the action. It is the outcome of a particular course of action or state.

When God gave man the freedom to choose, man also became responsible for the consequences of his decisions. His decision to eat from the forbidden tree was simultaneously a decision to die. Decisions and consequences go hand in hand. Every choice we make in life comes packaged with values, whether intended or not.

One of the wonders and conveniences of our day is the GPS. We input destinations we want to go to, then it plots a path to the destination, taking us through roads that have fixed beginning and ending points. Decisions are like roads. They lead somewhere. If you are in Chicago and you get on I-94 North, and you keep going, you will arrive at the north suburbs of Chicago, and if you don't stop, you will end up in Wisconsin, not Indiana. Decisions are like that. They are paths to predetermined destinations.

If you look at your life now, where you are now is a consequence of decisions you made in the past, and where you will be is predicated on the decisions you are making now. There is no escaping that fact. Your life is a sum of your choices. You chose to be educated; that's why you have the degree. You chose the person you are married to, and all that comes with that choice are consequences. You chose your thoughts. They became your habits. Your habits became your character, and your character becomes your destiny. Decisions are like seeds. They grow up to become plants that produce fruit. That is why Paul says "Do not be deceived: God cannot be mocked. A man reaps what he sows" (Galatians 6:7). This is the law of consequence.

What will you do with this truth of consequences? First, accept that everything that surrounds you in life now is nobody else's primary responsibility, whether good or bad. Take responsibility. If you are up to your head in debt, take responsibility. If your marriage or relationships are falling apart, take ownership. If you are in jail, take responsibility.

Stop pointing fingers at God, Satan, or others. Don't make the same mistake Adam and Eve made after eating from the tree, pointing fingers, "The Man said, "The Woman you gave me as a companion; she gave me fruit from the tree, and, yes, I ate it." God said to the Woman, "What is this that you've done?" "The serpent seduced me," she said, "and I ate." (Genesis 3:12-13 MSG). They were both transferring the blame.

Second, realize that God is a God of another chance. While the consequences of some decisions may be permanent, such as a child out of wedlock or a soiled reputation because of past actions, you still have the chance to make better decisions that will affect the overall destination of your life. If there is breath in you, there is hope. Life can begin anew from where you are now if you choose to make the right choices in line with the word of God. The first choice is to accept Him as your Lord if you haven't and to repent of your sins. Living in obedience to God's word is a choice and has consequences. Consequences you won't regret.

Decision of the Day

I understand that choices come with consequences. I accept that where I am in life now is a sum of my past decisions. I take responsibility. No one is to blame but me. I trust God with my past and future, and I will begin to make the right decisions based on His Word from this day. Lord, I rely on your grace.

| DAY 26

PARTNERSHIP

The Lord God said, "It is not good for the man to be alone. I will make a helper suitable for him."

Genesis 2:18

Scientists have observed that geese fly using a "V" pattern to make their flights easier. This formation allows each goose in flight to have an equal field of vision as the rest. A goose leads the formation, doing most of the work, but when it becomes tired, it moves to the back, and another goose takes its place in front.

This rotation continues through their flight and, as such, serves to conserve energy. Another advantage of the V flight pattern is that as each goose flaps its wings, it creates additional uplift for the bird immediately following. If one goose falls out of the formation, it immediately feels a drag that moves it to rejoin the group.

Also, if one of the birds falls ill or gets shot and falls out of the formation, two other birds will follow it down to aid it until it either recovers or dies and then rejoin the formation. The geese behind also honk to encourage the ones in front to keep pace. This is just one of the examples of the power of partnership.

So far, God has assessed His creative work and judged that everything was good. Then after creating Adam, He concluded that something was missing. The man lacked a suitable companion. This prompted a statement that reveals a lot about another critical component of maximized humanity- the necessity of partnership.

The statement "It is not good that the man be alone" has been interpreted by some to mean that God meant that Adam was lonely, so Eve had to be created to cure His loneliness. This is not what the verse means. Adam was not lonely. He was in the presence of God. He had a purpose for living. He had his assignment from God, and The wonderful provisions of God surrounded him. Loneliness is not the absence of companions; it is the absence of direction. It is possible to have many people surrounding you, in a relationship with you, and yet still be lonely.

The Hebrew word used for "alone" here means to be "only himself" or to be "all one," meaning it is not good for Adam to have all that God has provided from Him in the creation and to carry out the assignment He has received from God by Himself alone. He needed someone like him to share the blessings and responsibilities with him – a helpmeet. God was essentially saying that He did not create man to function alone.

Humanity was created for community. He was not to be a lone ranger or recluse. Man would only be able to reach the fullness of His potential as he links up with other humans in partnership. One is too small to achieve significance. We need partners to maximize life.

How about you? Are you a lone ranger? Do you have the mistaken belief that you can go it alone in life or that you can be a "self-made" person? You weren't created to function in isolation. In your life journey, you will need input from other individuals. You will need assistance from others no matter how gifted you are. Whatever idea or vision God has given you will require the partnership of others; that is why you need to cultivate relationships intentionally. Find like-minded people that can partner with you in that vision. Be part of an authentic community where there is openness and vulnerability. Start connecting with the visions of other people. Always remember that wholesome relationships are an essential part of your life, and you must be intentional in initiating and cultivating them.

Decision of the Day

I understand that God created me to partner with other people in the fulfillment of His plans for me. I cannot fulfill it alone. I need to link up with others and support them and be willing to receive support from them. From today, I will intentionally develop relationships, always making it a duty to be part of a community of authentic people.

| DAY 27

BONE OF MY BONES

"So the Lord God caused the man to fall into a deep sleep. While the man slept, the Lord God took out one of the man's ribs and closed up the opening. Then the Lord God made a woman from the rib, and he brought her to the man. "At last!" the man exclaimed. "This one is bone from my bone, and flesh from my flesh! She will be called 'woman,' because she was taken from 'man. This explains why a man leaves his father and mother and is joined to his wife, and the two are united into one. This explains why a man leaves his father and mother and is joined to his wife, and the two are united into one. Now the man and his wife were both naked, but they felt no shame."

- Genesis 2:21-25

The first institution God established after He made man was the family. It is the most important institution. It is the foundation of human society. Every other institution will take its root from the family. The state of families will determine the success or collapse of society.

ORDER FROM CHAOS

The good and the ill in society can be traced back to the family. Therefore, Satan's worst attacks are against the family institution. Families grow out of marriage. So, the beginning of the family institution is the marriage institution. In our text today, we see some truths about the first marriage and some good advice for those trusting God for a spouse.

The first thing we see is that God is a matchmaker. While Adam was sleeping, He created Eve and then brought her to Adam, who woke up to exclaim in delight at seeing his wife. God is still a matchmaker. If you are single and trusting God for a mate, meditating on what He did in arranging the first marriage could help you. Ponder on the following truths:

1. He put Adam into a deep sleep. Even though this was talking about a literal deep sleep, a deep figurative sleep would do much good for anyone searching for a mate. Commit your situation to God's hand and sleep deeply from your fears, worries, and concerns. Cast your cares on the Lord and let Him do what only He can do.

2. He made Eve. Trust that God is making someone for you right now (not that He is just creating the person!). In the same way, God is working on you right now and changing different aspects of your life to make you a better person; God is working on your mate where they are too.

3. He brought them together. God orchestrates relationships. He arranges divine appointments. God can direct people to move from one location to another to accomplish His plans. In Acts 8, Phillip was directed and transported to a particular place because He needed to meet the Ethiopian eunuch. It was a divine arrangement. Stay where God wants you to be, or go where He leads you and be expectant because your future spouse will be coming around.

4. He presented Eve to Adam. When it comes to the issue of marital partners, God makes presentations and expects you to make your choice. Adam said, "this is now bone of my bones and flesh of my flesh." Look around you now. Are there presentations that God is making to you? Examine your circle of relationships right now, and be sensitive to God's prompting as you meet people. Your sweetheart might be already around you. They might even be a that close friend of yours or that person you are constantly running into.

5. Bone of your bones: How did Adam identify his spouse? In his little poetry of joy, he tells us, "this is now bone of my bones..." He found something in her that they had in common, even though they were different people. Your prospective spouse will be different from you, but there will be some identifiable things to you that you have in common. Things like your faith and sharing a complementary purpose should not be compromised. "Can two walk together except they agree?"(Amos 3:3). Paul also warned about unequal yokes (2 Corinthians 6:14).

6. Marriage involves leaving and cleaving. The man and the woman are to leave their parents and cleave to each other in marriage. Even though you may not have found a spouse now, or you have found one but are still courting, it is never too early to start the process of leaving. Focus on achieving financial and emotional independence from your parents or other people. Keep moving forward in God's purpose for you. Get more educated if you need to. Don't sit waiting for a spouse to do stuff with your life. If you keep moving, you are likely to meet someone who is also moving.

And if you are already married, there's something here for you too. The purpose of your marriage is a union under God for a unique assignment for you and your spouse. Preserve that union. Deal with things that try to separate you and isolate you. Let nothing or no one come in between you. Preserve and increase the "one flesh" status of your marriage.

Decision of the Day

I understand that God is the author of marriage, and He wants to be a partner with me in having a successful family. He is a divine orchestrator and matchmaker. He is a uniter. I will commit my marital situations into His hand today and trust Him for the best.

| DAY 28

THE ANATOMY OF TEMPTATION

"The woman was convinced. She saw that the tree was beautiful and its fruit looked delicious, and she wanted the wisdom it would give her. So she took some of the fruit and ate it. Then she gave some to her husband, who was with her, and he ate it, too."

- Genesis 3:6 NLT

A temptation is a solicitation to do something that strongly appeals to one of our senses. A temptation to sin is an appeal to do something forbidden by God's word. The temptation of Adam and Eve in our text today is an example that illustrates all the various elements of a typical temptation.

1. There is a Boundary: Something interesting about the boundaries of God is that they are not there to keep us from enjoying life. They are there to keep us from ruining the good life He has planned for us. Adam and Eve had all the other trees they could eat from, including the tree of life, which could give their bodies immortality. Instead of eating that more beneficial tree, the tempter fixated their attention on the forbidden one. Isn't this still what is happening today? You have heard of many individuals who may have been blessed in life wonderfully: a great spouse, a wonderful family, a great career or ministry, but who messed up the whole thing by yielding to the temptation to go after one forbidden pleasure.

2. There is a Tempter. Why is this important to know? At the moment of temptation, it usually seems that we are the only one present and then the thing we are tempted to do. We, however, need to know that a puppet master is pulling the strings of the temptation. He is the devil. In his subtlety, he loves to hide, either to make you believe he is not there or that he has your good at heart. His power is deception, but his goal is your destruction. Also, remember that God is there to help you overcome, and He is not the tempter.

3. Everyone Will be Tempted. Adam and Eve were perfect. That had no form of evil in them. They lived in God's garden and presence, yet they were tempted. Never get to a point where you think you are too strong to be tempted. Heed the warning of Paul, "let him who thinks he stands, take heed lest he falls" (1 Corinthians 10:12)

4. There is an Atmosphere: Martin Luther once said, "Don't sit near the fire if your head is made of butter."

Temptations have more power when something in us aligns with the object of temptation, and the atmosphere is conducive. When Satan tempted Jesus in Luke 4 and failed, he left him to come back "at an opportune time." Satan looks for opportunities, the optimal atmosphere to tempt. It may be a moment of loneliness or solitude, being with the wrong friends, or watching or listening to bad things.

Therefore, one of the antidotes to temptation is to flee all appearances of evil (1 Thessalonians 5:22). Mark Twain said, "There are several good protections against temptation, but the surest is cowardice." Avoid putting yourself in tempting situations. Run from it. Pray that you do not fall into temptation as Jesus taught us. Keep yourself saturated with the word of God.

5. There is a Suggestion. Temptations are suggestions. Like the serpent's discussion with Eve, the suggestion calls your attention to crossing a boundary. These suggestions come as thoughts in your mind. Sometimes it seems you are deliberating with someone or yourself. Thoughts float through your mind: "Is God's word really true?" "wouldn't it be fun to do that" "I don't think God would want to stop me from enjoying that," "I can always repent," "everyone is doing it," "Just once won't hurt," "Just this last time" "No one will know," "No one will be hurt" or "I'm already bad, so it doesn't make any difference." These thoughts are usually lies or false promises.

ORDER FROM CHAOS

These suggestions then make the appeal stronger.

6. There is an Action: A temptation is not a sin. It is only when temptation is acted on that it becomes one. There are two sets of responses to temptation: resistance or compliance. A successful temptation is one that you yield to. An unsuccessful one is the one that you resist. The Bible tells us that God will never allow temptation we cannot handle and that even in the heat of temptations, God provides a way of escape (1 Corinthians 10:13).

Your responsibility is to take the way of escape, which is to look to God for the strength and grace to run away from the enormously appealing suggestions, to cast out thoughts and imaginations, or to reach out to someone, such as a trusted friend or mentor, who can help you at that moment. Also, you can resist temptation as Jesus did by speaking the word out against temptation.

7. There is a Consequence. Yielding to or resisting temptations have consequences. In the case of Adam and Eve, it was shame, regret, and significant loss. It is still the same now. Every time you yield to temptations, you lose something. Something dies in you. God's presence is grieved, and you lose your fellowship with Him with the consequences. You also become more susceptible to further temptations with every yes you say to it. Resisting temptations has rewards too. The more you say no, the less power the appeal has on you in the future, and the blessing of obedience comes into your lives.

If you are struggling with a particular temptation or have just fallen into one, remember that God loves you and wants to help you. Jesus tasted temptation while He was on the earth, and He is now your faithful high priest who can sympathize with your feelings. Run to Him in prayer for mercy and grace (Hebrews 4:16). He will forgive and strengthen you.

Decision of the Day

I will run to the throne of grace today for mercy and grace to overcome temptation. I will run from all appearances of evil and not put myself in situations where I can be easily tempted.

| DAY 29

THE GOOD NEWS

"The woman was convinced. She saw that the tree was beautiful and its fruit looked delicious, and she wanted the wisdom it would give her. So she took some of the fruit and ate it. Then she gave some to her husband, who was with her, and he ate it, too. At that moment their eyes were opened, and they suddenly felt shame at their nakedness. So they sewed fig leaves together to cover themselves...Then the Lord God called to the man, "Where are you? He replied, "I heard you walking in the garden, so I hid. I was afraid because I was naked."

- Genesis 3:6-10 NLT

Sometimes, closed eyes are better than open ones. It is better to have your eyes closed to the ravages of drugs on your body than have your eyes opened to them through personal experience. It is better not to have been exposed to pornography than for you to be struggling with the consequences of exposure. Lord, please close our eyes to things they shouldn't be opened to.

Sin is a disease. It has symptoms. Sin never comes alone. It comes with its wage, death (Romans 6:23). This is not just speaking of physical death, but separation from God. Death is the absence of Life. God is Life. In Him is the fountain that brings rest, peace, faith, health, abundance, creativity and all the good things in life. In His absence, all that is left is a gaping hole of darkness and misery.

Adam and Eve had lived this Life, and they had been surrounded by the fullness of all that is good. They lived in the garden of delight. They were rulers of earth saturated with the blessings of God. They were creative, confident, and bold. They were peaceful and full of joy and purpose.

They were naked and not ashamed because they had the glory of God on them. Then sin came. They yielded to temptations and disobeyed God. God had warned them that the moment they broke, they would die. Died, they did. They became separated from God, who is Life, and they immediately began to manifest the symptoms of sin.

1. They saw they were naked and were ashamed
2. They became afraid
3. They hid from God
4. They covered themselves with leaves

This was the entrance of sin consciousness into the world. Sin still strips us of God's glory and leaves us naked, ashamed, and afraid. We run from God's presence that we used to love, and rather than being covered with His glory, we try to cover ourselves with leaves of self-righteousness and good works. We forget the grace and start to depend on dead works. Sin brings condemnation and fear. This disease afflicts the whole world, for all have sinned and fallen short of the glory of God (Romans 3:23).

The good news is that the story did not end there. Jesus Christ, the only cure for sin, came into the world with His substitutionary death—the only antidote to sin. Through death, He conquered sin and death and opened our access to Life again. The reason why Jesus came was to destroy the works of the devil (I John 3:8) and to reverse the consequences of the fall of man.

Through Him, sin died. Sin consciousness is purged from our hearts. Righteousness, which is the sense of guiltlessness and confidence in God's presence, is restored to those who accept His work and believe in Him. He is the Way back to the father's presence, the Truth, and the Life. He is our righteousness, the Lamb who was slain to reconcile us to God.

Are you living in sin consciousness? Do you have a conscience that is constantly condemning you, making you afraid of God? Are you living in guilt over some past or present sins of your life? You don't need to live this way again. Rather than running from Him and hiding, run to Him. Run into His arm. Call on Jesus to heal you, purge you of your guilt, cleanse your guilty conscience and give you His righteousness. Joy, confidence, and peace can come back into your life. You can breathe in the presence of life again.

Decision of the Day

I know Jesus died to free me from sin and its consequences. His blood can purge my conscience from the consciousness of sin. I don't need to hide from God in condemnation and fear. He loves me and has made provisions for me to be forgiven and cleansed of my sins. I will look to Him today and receive His righteousness, relinquishing all self-effort to cleanse myself. I will trust in His grace.

| DAY 30

TAKE RESPONSIBILITY

"The man replied, "It was the woman you gave me who gave me the fruit, and I ate it." Then the Lord God asked the woman, "What have you done?" "The serpent deceived me," she replied. "That's why I ate it."

- Genesis 3:12-13 NLT

I once saw a cartoon from Randy Glasbergen in which a guy was asked what was made at his workplace. He quickly replied, "we make excuses." That is a joke, of course, but there is some truth to it. There is always some explanation for every failure or inability to fulfill our responsibilities.

The habit of making excuses is one that is prevalent. The blame usually falls elsewhere: a spouse, some circumstances, background, lack of money, the in-laws, past abuse, or the nation's economy. Remember the classic excuse of children who didn't get their homework done, "my dog ate it."

In our text today, we see Adam and Eve pointing fingers and making excuses after disobeying God's command. The man blamed the woman and God who gave him the woman. The woman blamed the serpent that God had made. In essence, they were pointing fingers at God and the devil.

Isn't that what we still do today? Rather than taking personal responsibility for the things that occur in our lives, knowing that we were given choices and our choices led to outcomes, we blame God, the devil, and circumstances.

The devil tempts us, but it is true that he can't make us do anything. He can't force our choices. We are responsible for what we think, say, and eventually do. In James 1: 13-15, we read, "And remember, when you are being tempted, do not say, "God is tempting me." God is never tempted to do wrong and never tempts anyone else.

Temptation comes from our desires, enticing and dragging us away. These desires give birth to sinful actions. And when sin is allowed to grow, it gives birth to death." in other words, don't blame God. Take responsibility.

There are indeed some events in your life that you cannot control or take responsibility for their occurrence: natural disasters, death of loved ones, the weather, the political and economic climate of the nation, your background and upbringing, disabilities you were born with and a host of others. However, you are not responsible

ORDER FROM CHAOS

for the occurrences of these things; you are still in charge of your response to them.

It is not the events of life that determine your outcomes. It is your response to the events of life that determines your result. Two individuals can face the same circumstances, one with thankfulness, faith, and reliance on God, squeezing life's lemons into lemonade. In contrast, the other faces the same events with fear, doubt, and complaining.

They will have different outcomes. That was the case in Numbers 13 and 14, when Moses sent out the twelve spies to spy out the promised land. They all saw the same things, but their responses to what they saw were different. Ten saw giants they could not conquer, while two, Caleb and Joshua, saw themselves as being able to overcome in God. The outcome? The ten died in the wilderness, while Caleb and Joshua went on to conquer lands and mountains. Your response determines your outcome.

Decide today to take responsibility for your life. Stop blaming others. No one is to blame. You have no excuse for failure but the excuses themselves. If you don't like your outcome, change your responses. You have control over yourself, the thoughts you think, the words you speak, the relationships you keep, whether you exercise or overspend, the food you eat, the decisions you make, and your behaviors and actions. Quit complaining about life and how it has handed you the short end of the stick. You have a God whose hand is not shortened even if it has.

Change your responses. Respond with faith and trust in Him. He will help you.

Decision of the Day

I understand that I am responsible for 100 percent of my life. Everything in my life now is my responsibility. I quit pointing fingers and blaming others. Instead, I will respond in faith, even when life hands me negative situations. My response is what determines my outcome, not the events of my life.

| DAY 31

TWO FORCES

"And to the man he said, "Since you listened to your wife and ate from the tree whose fruit I commanded you not to eat, the ground is cursed because of you. All your life you will struggle to scratch a living from it. It will grow thorns and thistles for you, though you will eat of its grains..."

- Genesis 3:17-18 NLT

In August 2005, Hurricane Katrina, one of the five deadliest in the History of the United States, descended over several states including Louisiana claiming hundreds of lives and leaving behind billions of dollars in damages, broken hearts, and wounded communities.

In our text today, we see the introduction of a new reality on the earth. A new force, malevolent in nature, contrary to what was in operation so far on the earth, came into operation as a consequence of disobedience to God, And like a hurricane, it would leave destruction, misery, pain, sorrow, and decay in its path.

A force is an influence that produces effects when it exerts itself on a thing. Two forces are mentioned throughout the bible, the blessing and the curse. The curse is what came into operation from the time Adam sinned.

In our text, God pronounced some of its destructive effects. It is the opposite of a blessing. It is the absence of the blessing. Whenever it is operational on an entity, it brings sorrow, sadness, losses, diseases, struggles, failures, diminishing returns, troubles, stagnancy, and calamities. It continues to work to destroy whatever entity it is on (Read Deuteronomy 28:15-end) to see some of the curse's effects.

On the other hand, the blessing is a benevolent and positive influence of God that acts on people, places, and things and moves them toward fruitfulness, increase, multiplication, and dominion. When an entity is blessed, it possesses the power to grow and succeed. The blessing has in it the ability to change negative situations into positive ones, to raise people from the dunghill, to protect, cause them to excel and make progress, to give wisdom, to heal, multiply, favor, and to make rich (Proverbs 10:22).

The blessing is not physical, like money, cars, houses, promotions, ministry effectiveness, family peace and rest, etc. Those could be the effects of the blessing. It is an invisible spiritual influence that produces tangible physical effects. It is like the wind, which is invisible but whose effects can be seen as trees and objects sway at its passing.

The blessing was put on Adam and Eve at creation. "And God blessed them, and God said unto them, "Be fruitful, and multiply, and replenish the earth, and subdue it: and have dominion..." (Genesis 1:28)

The blessing was upon Abraham "And I will make of thee a great nation, and I will bless thee, and make thy name great; and thou shalt be a blessing: And I will bless them that bless you and curse him that curses you: and in you shall all families of the earth be blessed." (Genesis 12:2, 3). And, "Abraham was old, [and] well stricken in age: and the Lord had blessed Abraham in all things." (Genesis 24:1)

It was on Isaac "Then Isaac sowed in that land, and received in the same year a hundredfold: and the Lord blessed him. And the man waxed great, and went forward, and grew until he became very great: For he had possession of flocks, and possession of herds, and great store of servants: and the Philistines envied him." (Genesis 26:12-14)

It was on Jacob. "And Isaac called Jacob, and blessed him, and charged him, and said unto him... And God Almighty bless thee, and make thee fruitful, and multiply thee, that thou mayest be a multitude of people; And give thee the blessing of Abraham, to thee, and thy seed with thee; that thou mayest inherit the land wherein thou art a stranger, which God gave unto Abraham." Genesis 28:1-4

It was on Joseph. "And the Lord was with Joseph, and he was a prosperous man, and he was in the house of his master, the Egyptian. And his master saw that the Lord [was] with him, and that the LORD made all that he did to prosper in his hand. And it came to pass from the time [that] he had made him overseer in his house, and over all that he had, that the Lord blessed the Egyptian's house for Joseph's sake; and the blessing of the LORD was upon all that he had in the house, and in the field." (Genesis 39:1-5)

It was on the nation of Israel as they obeyed God. "And it shall come to pass, if thou shalt hearken diligently unto the voice of the Lord thy God, to observe [and] to do all his commandments which I command thee this day, that the LORD thy God will set thee on high above all nations of the earth: And all these blessings shall come on thee, and overtake thee if thou shalt hearken unto the voice of the Lord thy God." (Deuteronomy 28:1, 2)

It was on Jesus, "And she spoke out with a loud voice, and said, Blessed, are you among women, and blessed [is] the fruit of your womb." (Luke 1:4)

It is on His body. "Christ has redeemed us from the curse of the law, being made a curse for us: for it is written, cursed [is] every one that is hung on a tree: That the blessing of Abraham might come on the Gentiles through Jesus Christ; that we might receive the promise of the Spirit through faith." (Galatians 3:13-14)

It is on you. "Blessed [be] the God and Father of our Lord Jesus Christ, who has blessed us with all spiritual blessings in heavenly [places] in Christ" (Ephesians 1:3). The blessing comes from obeying and putting faith in God's word. The curse comes because of disobedience and distrust in God's word. Israel alternated between being blessed and being cursed all through their biblical history. When blessed, they prospered and conquered the nations around them. When cursed, they were devastated and taken into captivity.

In the New Testament, Jesus became your substitute. Your relationship with God is based on Him. You are in Christ. So, because He obeyed the Father to the point of death, He is forever blessed, and you are in Him. So, He legally redeemed you from the curse (Galatians 3:13-14). He has made the blessing available to you. By trusting and exercising conscious faith in this blessing, you enter the fullness of the force of the blessing.

You become fruitful, healthy, victorious, more than a conqueror, and bold. You become a great influencer of people and places. You can take this force into situations and areas of darkness, and things begin to change through your presence. It is the same blessing that was on Abraham that is on you. God told Abraham, "Through you, all the families of the earth will be blessed."

People, families, industries, communities, neighborhoods, and nations should be blessed through believers walking in conscious faith in the blessing.

You are blessed in Christ. Believe it! Declare it! You are blessed to be a blessing. This is not just a cliché. It is reality. There is an influence on you from God to assist you in your living and calling. It eliminates the curse just as light dissolves darkness. It can illuminate your mind and give you wisdom, strategies, and ideas for progress. It opens closed doors. It ensures uncommon supernatural provisions, healing, and restoration.

The apostles had it, and they spread it. It is still here because the Holy Spirit is still here. Crave this blessing like Jacob and Esau craved it and plotted for it. It will not work automatically because the switch of faith activates it. It is like electricity. It can be invisibly present in the wall outlet, but nothing happens until you flip the switch. Flip the switch.

Believe the report of the Lord. Walk with blessed people. Bless blessed people. Declare His goodness in your life. Speak the word of God over your body, mind, family, children, career, or ministry. God's word carries the blessing, and He wants you blessed to be a blessing so that His purpose of filling the earth with His glory can be accomplished. It is your choice to walk in the blessing. "I call heaven and earth to record this day against you, [that] I have set before you life and death, blessing and cursing: therefore, choose life, that both thou and thy seed may live:" (Deuteronomy 30:19)

Decision of the Day

I understand that the blessing is a force of good from God. It is available to me. It is my choice to walk in the blessing or the curse. I choose the blessing. I will keep it activated in my life by faith. I will walk with the blessed and I will see the effects of the blessing increasing in my life, family, calling, and community to the glory of God.

| DAY 32
IS THIS THE BEST I CAN DO?

"When it was time for the harvest, Cain presented some of his crops as a gift to the Lord. Abel also brought a gift— the best of the firstborn lambs from his flock. The Lord accepted Abel and his gift, but he did not accept Cain and his gift. This made Cain very angry, and he looked dejected. "Why are you so angry?" the Lord asked Cain. "Why do you look so dejected? You will be accepted if you do what is right. But if you refuse to do what is right, then watch out! Sin is crouching at the door, eager to control you. But you must subdue it and be its master."

- Genesis 4:3-7 NLT

Henry Kissinger, the former US Secretary of States and Nobel laureate, tells a story in his book, The Whitehouse Years: A Harvard professor handling back to students the papers of an assignment they had turned in wrote at the bottom of one "Is this the best you can do?" The student decided to redo the paper and turned it in again. The professor returned it to him with the same words written underneath it. "Is this the best you can do?" This happened ten times until the student returned the paper and said," Yes, this is the best I can do." Then the professor replied, "Fine, now I'll read it."

Today's story in our text is one that theologians have debated for a long time. The central question has been, "Why was Cain's offering rejected by God and Abel's accepted?" Several reasons have been given, such as "Abel offered an offering of blood, but Cain did not," " Abel offered the firstlings of his flocks, while Cain offered just part of his harvest," or Abel offered in faith, while Cain did not." Our intention today is not to say that there is only one reason why his offering was rejected since it may be for a host of reasons best known to God.

However, by studying this story and other parts of the scriptures, we can learn a lot about giving to God. Here are some lessons we can take away today.

1. God loves our gifts. God doesn't need anything from you since He is all-sufficient, but He is pleased when you come to Him and give back to Him in appreciation and acknowledgment of His blessings in your life. The New Testament says, "He loves cheerful givers." It pleases Him when you show gratitude and respond to His benevolence with praise, worship, and your gifts.

2. God does not accept every gift, implying that he has standards. Just like the Harvard professor in the story,

He does not just accept anything. He has his criteria for acceptance. You cannot just give anything to God. The only gifts He will receive are those that meet His criteria. So, what are some of God's criteria as revealed in the scriptures?

First, for a gift to be acceptable to God, the giver must be acceptable to God. Our story tells us that Cain and His offerings were rejected. It was not just the offering but Cain too that was rejected. There was something in Cain that made his offering repulsive to God. We have some hints. Hebrews 11.4 implies that Cain did not give his offering in faith and 1 John 3.12 says that He had evil intentions.

God wants us to give with the right attitude. The motivation behind our giving matters a lot. We are told to give cheerfully and not grudgingly or out of compulsion (2 Corinthians 9:7). We are instructed not to give to impress others but to make our gifts a secret between ourselves and God (Matthew 6:1-4). We are also to give with an attitude of gratitude and praise.

Perhaps, one of the greatest lessons of the story is in the quality of gifts they gave. Abel gave the best of his firstborn lambs from God, while Cain is said to have given just some of his crops. The differentiation in the quality of their gifts is not accidental, but it was meant to be a lesson to us. The practice of giving the first fruit was institutionalized in the law by Moses, the writer of Genesis and the story of Cain and Abel. This was probably included to show that the practice predates the law. It is a principle.

God deserves the first and the best from us. God does not want leftovers. He wants the first and the best. "Honor the Lord with your wealth and with the best part of everything you produce. Then he will fill your barns with grain, and your vats will overflow with good wine." (Proverbs 3:10-11).

Will you decide today to give God your best this new year? First, the best of yourself: your heart, your devotion, your strength, talents, and commitment to Him. Then will you give Him the best of your possessions: your time, money, and treasures?

Love, worship, and praise Him with all your heart, soul, and strength. Whenever you are doing anything for God, ask yourself, "Is this the best I can do?" if your answer is yes, then do it joyfully; if it is no, then up your act. God deserves the best from you.

Decision of the Day

I understand that God deserves the best of me and from me. I give him my whole self this year. I will provide him with the best of my possessions. He will always be first in my life.

| DAY 33

BROTHER'S KEEPER

Then the Lord said to Cain, "Where is your brother Abel?" "I don't know," he replied. "Am I my brother's keeper?"

- Genesis 4:9 NLT

In one of Aesop's fables, *The Three Tradesmen*, He tells this story about a great city under attack. The city's inhabitants were called together to figure out a way to best defend the town. A Bricklayer was the first to stand up, earnestly recommending bricks as the best material for the defense.

After him, a Carpenter, with equal zeal, proposed timber as the preferable method of protecting the city. Then the Leather maker stood up and said: " Sirs, I disagree with you both: there is no better material for defense than a covering of leather." This fable illustrates the popular idiom, "everyman for himself."

In our text today, God asked Cain a question, and he replied with another. These two questions contain some important lessons for us when viewed from the lens of other parts of the scriptures. God's question, "where is your brother...?" was one of responsibility. It implies that Cain was expected to know where his brother was. Even though it was a lie, Cain's response was meant to convey indifference and non-culpability for what happened to his brother.

The Bible tells us that Christianity has two main focuses, loving God and loving our neighbors. That is what all the commandments of the Bible boil down to, according to Jesus (Matthew 22:38). Even though the Bible teaches individual responsibility and that each of us will give an account of himself to God (Romans 14:12), "every man for himself" is not a scriptural motto that we can adopt.

Part of the account you will have to give are the opportunities to be a blessing to some people God has attached to your life. You have some responsibilities to your neighbors. You are to be your brother's keeper.

The idea of a keeper is not to take over people's responsibilities, subsidize their laziness, or make decisions for them and protect them from the consequences of their choices. Instead, it is to lovingly assist others as they try to carry out their responsibilities in life. It is to live your life with an awareness that you are not the only one on the planet, that there are others that you were placed here to help.

Look at some of the commands of scriptures about our responsibilities to our neighbors.

1. Be interested: Philippians 2:4, "Don't look out only for your own interests, but take an interest in others, too."

2. Pray. "Confess your sins to each other and pray for each other so that you may be healed..." (James 5:16)

3. Restore: "Dear brothers and sisters, if another believer is overcome by some sin, you who are godly should gently and humbly help that person back onto the right path..." (Galatians 6:1)

4. Don't cause others to fall. "But you must be careful so that your freedom does not cause others with a weaker conscience to stumble." (1 Corinthians 8:9)

5. Give: "If someone has enough money to live well and sees a brother or sister in need but shows no compassion—how can God's love be in that person?" (I John 3:17).
"Suppose you see a brother or sister who has no food or clothing, and you say, "Good-bye and have a good day; stay warm and eat well"—but then you don't give that person any food or clothing. What good does that do?" (James 2:15-16)

6. Be Kind: "Add to your faith...brotherly kindness. (2 Peter 1:7)

7. Encourage and motivate: Let us think of ways to motivate one another to acts of love and good works. (Hebrews 10:25)

8. Warn: "Take note of those who refuse to obey what we say in this letter. Stay away from them so they will be ashamed. Don't think of them as enemies but warn them as you would a brother or sister." (1 Thessalonians 3:14-15)

This is practical Christianity. Decide today to live a life that is not focused on your self-interest alone, as illustrated by the three tradesmen in the fable. Be one of those who will live for a cause greater than themselves. In doing that, you will be obeying and imitating your master, the keeper who died for you.

Decision of the Day

I understand that I am placed here on earth by God, not just to live for myself. I am here to assist others too. I renounce selfish living, and I will begin to obey the command of Christ to love my neighbors as myself by taking advantage of the opportunities God has surrounded me with to love and assist others.

| DAY 34

A HIGHER REALM

"When Enoch had lived 65 years, he became the father of Methuselah. After he became the father of Methuselah, Enoch walked faithfully with God 300 years and had other sons and daughters. Altogether, Enoch lived a total of 365 years. Enoch walked faithfully with God; then he was no more, because God took him away."

- Genesis 5:21-24 NLT

The story of Enoch is tucked in a part of the bible that sometimes could be difficult to read. In tracing the genealogy of Noah from Adam, we are taken through several lives, many relatively unremarkable, until we get to Enoch. Then the writer paused and commented on Enoch's life. He walked faithfully with God for 300 years. Here are some lessons from the story of this remarkable life.

1. **He didn't start life walking with God**. According to the text, something happened to Enoch at the age of 65

after the birth of his son Methuselah which sparked his faithful walk with God. We are not told what it was, but we can learn something from it.

God can use some events in your life to spark a desire for a renewed relationship with Him. It could be meeting someone, a spouse, the birth of a child, deliverance from a terrible situation, an unpleasant situation you just went through or are going through, or any other event. You need to be aware that God can turn every situation out for your good and His greatest good is for you to draw close to Him. Is there something going on in your life that God is using to nudge you to come closer to Him?

2. Enoch walked consistently with God. It is an encouragement to you that sustaining a consistent walk with God in life is possible. Hebrews 11 tells us that this walk of Enoch was one of faith. He dared to believe in God. He chose to go against the grains during his day. It was a time when the world was filled with corruption, and humans did not give regard to God.

Yet during all that, He chose to stay in tune with God, developing a friendship with Him. If Enoch could do it, then you can too. You can be consistent in your walk with God no matter the prevailing culture around you.

3. God took Him. Enoch became the first individual to experience the rapture because of His walk with God. He had walked so closely with God that one day, God decided that He so much enjoyed Enoch's company that He translated him from this physical realm into His realm to be with Him forever.

We are not promised a personal rapture like this but choosing to walk with God can take you into a realm beyond the natural. There is a higher realm in life that God is calling you to- a realm of intimacy, a place of fellowship, a place where though you live in this world, you are raised above the mundane pursuits of life where others may dwell.

Your life takes on a new meaning. You live only for Christ, and knowing Him and His purpose for your life becomes your main preoccupation. It is a sacred place of holy communion that God has reserved for you.

Determine to press into this new realm of living today. It comes by pursuit. God wants to walk with you. He wants a more intimate relationship with you too. He wants you to come closer. He wants you to leave the place of knowing about Him to knowing Him truly. It starts with reading His word and honoring it, fellowshipping with Him in prayer, and crying out to Him from the depth of your heart. As you spend quality time with Him in quantity, He will transform your life. You will not be disappointed.

Decision of the Day

I am determined to walk with God for the rest of my days. I desire to enter a more intimate relationship with God. I will follow this desire with a commitment to seeking God and drawing nearer to Him each day.

| DAY 35

THE FAVOR OF GOD

But Noah found favor with the LORD.

- Genesis 6:8 NLT

I love the way Max Lucado says this in his book, *A Gentle Thunder*:

"There are many reasons God saves you: to bring glory to himself, to appease his justice, to demonstrate his sovereignty. But one of the sweetest reasons God saved you is because he is fond of you. He likes having you around. He thinks you are the best thing to come down the pike in quite a while...

If God had a refrigerator, your picture would be on it. If He had a wallet, your photo would be in it. He sends you flowers every spring and a sunrise every morning. Whenever you want to talk, He'll listen. He can live anywhere in the universe, and He chose your heart. And the Christmas gift he sent you in Bethlehem? Face it, friend. He's crazy about you!" [1]

ORDER FROM CHAOS

Although much of God's favor has been implied in various instances in the book of Genesis, it is first directly mentioned in the bible in our text today. This disposition of God toward specific individuals among humans runs as a theme throughout the bible and becomes the focus of the New Testament. Favor is a disposition to help or do good to someone. The entire human race was condemned to judgment because of their sins, but Noah was singled out for deliverance by God.

God's favor is expressed in many ways throughout the scriptures. Individuals, families, or nations were given special attention, singled out for good, exempted from judgment, chosen for important tasks, spotlighted, given special callings, made victorious over enemies, prospered, assisted to excellence, and granted special privileges because they had the favor of God directed toward them. The light of God's countenance shone on them.

However, of all these acts of favor from God, none compares with His most significant act of favor which He showed you in Christ when He sent Him to die for your sins and which you received when you accepted His salvation. "For it is by grace you have been saved, through faith—and this is not from yourselves, it is the gift of God—not by works, so that no one can boast." (Eph 2:8,9).

God chose you out of the graveyard of the world, raised you and breathed new life into you, and gave you a new nature and name. He adopted you into His family and now calls you son. "See what great love the Father has lavished on us, that we should be called children of God! And that is what we are... (I John 3:1).

God hasn't stopped loving you. His favor is still yours. If He loved you enough to die for you when you were still his enemy, how much more now that you are His child? "You see, at just the right time, when we were still powerless, Christ died for the ungodly.... But God demonstrates his own love for us in this: While we were still sinners, Christ died for us." (Romans 5:6-8).

You are the beloved of God. His favor is on your life because of Christ. Believe it! Cherish it! Declare it!

Decision of the Day

I thank God for His undeserved favor in my life. I believe in His love for me. I will walk in the consciousness of His favor and love for me today and always, expecting the manifestation of His special privileges in my life permanently.

| DAY 36

PERSISTENT FAITH

"So God said to Noah, "I am going to put an end to all people, for the earth is filled with violence because of them. I am surely going to destroy both them and the earth. So make yourself an ark of cypress wood; make rooms in it and coat it with pitch inside and out. This is how you are to build it: The ark is to be three hundred cubits long, fifty cubits wide, and thirty cubits high...Noah did everything just as God commanded him."

- Genesis 6:13-22 NIV

There is a story from the life of Robert and Mary Moffat, missionaries to Botswana (then called Bechuanaland). They had been laboring continually for ten years in the nation without any converts. Their mission board began to doubt whether they should continue the work and recommended returning to England. The couple was sad to leave their post, so they chose to stay, trusting God for fruits.

They did this for a couple of more years, still with no fruit. Then one day, they received a message from a friend in England who wanted to mail them a gift but wanted to know what they would like. Mary Moffat replied, "Send us a communion set; I am sure it will soon be needed," expressing her faith in God that they would soon have converts.

Soon, God blessed their work; they had six converts that met to form the first Christian church in Botswana. The communion sets, which were delayed in coming, arrived on the eve of the day of the first Lord's supper in Botswana. Robert Moffat translated the first Bible into the South African language. During a trip to England, he was the one who persuaded David Livingstone to come to Africa. David Livingstone, who became of the greatest missionaries to Africa, married the Moffat's daughter.

What a testimony of faith. The testimony of the Moffats is very similar to the testimony of God about Noah "By faith Noah, when warned about things not yet seen, in holy fear built an ark to save his family. By his faith he condemned the world and became heir of the righteousness that is in keeping with faith." (Hebrews 11:7).

Noah received an instruction from God to build an ark because a massive deluge was coming, and though he had not seen the rain yet, and it would be about another 100 years before the rain would come, he moved in response to the unseen and began building the ark. You can imagine the ridicule he must have endured through the years of building the ark. People must have laughed, mocked, and tagged him as a crazy old man. But Noah knew what He heard from God and persevered in obedience just as the Moffats did. Eventually, vindication came as God's word came to pass in their lives.

What have you heard from God that seems delayed? A calling, a spouse, children, a job, salvation of a loved one, a healed marriage? Have you been laboring for what seems such a long time on a ministry or vision that you know God gave you with little or no fruit? Don't quit.

Your continued obedience is your faith in God, and God honors faith. Don't let a lack of immediate results lead you to quit. Keep trusting. Keep loving. Stick to it! God will not fail in bringing His word to you to pass. And perhaps you are on the verge of stepping out to do something that God has instructed you to do, but nothing around you is favorable to your vision.

Don't look around. Don't be immobilized because you can't see anything. Step out on the word you have received. God will hold you. He will honor your faith. Your obedience is your faith.

Decision of the Day

I will not quit on the vision God has given me. I will hold on even through tough times. God will not fail in His promises to me. He honors faith. I will continue to obey Him by persisting, no matter how long I take. My vindication is on its way.

| DAY 37

MARANATHA

"A male and female of each kind entered, just as God had commanded Noah. Then the Lord closed the door behind them."

- Genesis 7:16 NLT

Whenever members of the early church met or parted, they did not greet one another with "hello," "hi," "goodbye," or "see you later." Instead, they said, "Maranatha." "Maranatha" is an Aramaic word meaning, "Our Lord comes," or "Come Oh, Lord." During the fierce persecutions they faced, they maintained hope by reminding themselves constantly of the promised return of the Lord Jesus Christ. They also kept their awareness of His coming to prevent themselves from getting caught up in the affairs of life and losing their attitude of watchfulness.

The Lord Jesus likened the events surrounding His second coming to what happened during the time of Noah.

ORDER FROM CHAOS

"When the Son of Man returns, it will be like it was in Noah's day. In those days before the flood, the people were enjoying banquets and parties and weddings right up to the time Noah entered his boat. People didn't realize what was going to happen until the flood came and swept them all away...So you, too, must keep watch! For you don't know what day your Lord is coming...You also must be ready all the time, for the Son of Man will come when least expected." (Matthew 24:37-44)

The judgment of God was imminent, yet the people were unaware. They were caught up in the festivities of life: partying, marrying, eating, and drinking until the judgment fell, and it was too late. Jesus warns us not to be like them but to be watchful because His return will be without warning and will happen when it is least expected.

It is straightforward to become so engrossed in the affairs of life that we begin to live with little or no awareness that our time on earth is wrapping up, whether by the return of the Lord or at the natural conclusions of our lives. The return of the Lord is a time of accountability, as the parables of Jesus show us. At His coming, the way you lived your life and how you managed the resources and opportunities He has given you will be evaluated as we see in the Parable of the Talents.

No one knows the time of His return, but it is imminent. It could be today or tomorrow. It could be any minute from now. A friend of mine told me a story of when their very old grandmother was in hospice care. Her departure was imminent, so the entire family was on alert. Everyone began to adjust their lives in preparation for the upcoming event of her passing away. Those who had not seen her in a while changed their schedules to see her before she died. Deliberations were made on her estate and so on. In the same way, understanding the imminent return of the Lord should spur you to live prepared.

First, you should ensure that you are ready for His coming by accepting the salvation He offers you through His death and resurrection. You should endeavor to live a holy life with His help. Live with a commitment to fulfilling your purpose on earth. Determine that even if He comes before you conclude your assignment, He will meet you actively pursuing it.

Live with a concern for the lost. Tell someone today of His coming and warn them that they must be prepared. God left you here to be His witness who blows the trumpet, announcing to all the truth of His imminent return. He has built an ark of salvation in Christ; now He wants you to be like Noah in your generation, who will fill the ark with the people He loves.

Finally, if you are going through persecutions, trials, or temptation, let the sure and soon coming of the Lord be an encouragement to you that it is all temporary. A new day is coming. Encourage yourself and others with this truth. Greet everyone with the joyful sound of Maranatha!

Decision of the Day

I know the return of the Lord is soon. I will live my life consistently with an awareness of this truth. I will be sober and watchful, actively pursuing His plans for me and looking forward to His coming with joy.

| DAY 38

SEASONS OF LIFE

"As long as the earth remains, there will be planting and harvest, cold and heat, summer and winter, day and night."

- Genesis 8:22 NLT

We are familiar with spring, summer, fall, and winter. Each of these seasons has its unique characteristics. Each has its demands. We clean the yard in spring, weed and tend the lawn in summer, clear the leaves in fall and clear the snow in winter. A year ends, another begins, and the seasons repeat their God-ordained cycle with predictable precision. We are no longer caught by surprise by the change in season. We are prepared. We are used to cycles.

According to our text today, God-ordained life on earth to run in continual cycles and seasons if it continues to exist. Seasons are permanent parts of life.

The cycles of life go beyond the weather. There are the planting and harvest season, sunrise and sunset, months, and years. There is childhood, youth, adulthood, and old age. There is birth, growth, and death. There will be seasons of pain and pleasure, seasons of sowing when there seems to be no harvest and reaping, seasons of laying foundations and then living in the edifice built, seasons of singleness and marriage, and seasons of childlessness and parenthood. Ecclesiastes 3:1 says everything in life has a season. "For everything, there is a season, a time for every activity under heaven."

You are in a season of your life right now, and soon, another is coming. Just like the cycles of the weather, each season of your life has unique characteristics, opportunities, and demands. Your part is to maximize the current season and prepare for the succeeding ones. Wherever you are in life today, childhood, youth, adulthood, midlife, or old age, there are advantages you should enjoy, opportunities to seize, and challenges to overcome.

Childhood and youth are like spring. They come with new opportunities to spread one's wings, soar, and blossom like flowers. If you are young, it is an opportunity to learn, dare, do, discover your place in life, and dive into your God-given passion with strength and vigor. It is a time for bold initiatives. Unfortunately, it could also be a time of distractions. Old age seems so far away and out of sight that precious time could be wasted on frivolities. Then comes adulthood, which is like summer. We are tending the seeds we've planted in the spring of youth, reaping some of the harvests. Life's responsibilities press on us like the hot sun, and we sweat.

Fall soon follows with its array of colors. The once bright things begin to fade. The hair turns gray, and the things that once stood tall in our bodies start to drop. Fall is an opportunity to enjoy the outdoors before winter comes.

It is a time to make up for some missed opportunities of summer. A time to wind down from the rigors of summer and to complete necessary preparations for winter. Time to make up with the children and grandchildren if there has been a rift. The last opportunity to get things stored for the previous season of life when mobility is limited because of winter.

Winter is the final season of life. It is hard outside, but it makes thoughts of home and its warmth pleasant. Winter is the time to huddle with the family around the fireplace of life, enjoying the warmth. Just as winter is when travels are made to places on earth with sunny weather, your old age is a time to enjoy the warmth of spring and summer again by sharing your life story and the wisdom you have gained with those still in spring. It is also time to make final preparation for departure from this realm of time, to set your house in order.

Whatever season you are in life, it can be fun and adventurous. You can be helpful. You can be joyful. Celebrate each season. Take advantage of the opportunities it offers you. Don't waste it because you are longing for another season. Use it to the full. It will soon pass.

Decision of the Day

I understand that my life is in seasons. I am in a season of life now full of opportunities. I will not waste the seasons. I will take full advantage of where I am currently in preparation for the next.

| DAY 39

YOU HAVE A COVENANT WITH GOD

"And God said, "This is the sign of the covenant I am making between me and you and every living creature with you, a covenant for all generations to come: I have set my rainbow in the clouds, and it will be the sign of the covenant between me and the earth."

- Genesis 9:12-13 NIV

To illustrate God's covenants, think of a benevolent and exceptionally resourced king who picks up a poor peasant and promises the peasant that he would give him half of His kingdom just as a favor.

Even though the king is known to never break his word- ever, after making the promise in the presence of all to the peasant, he then proceeds to make a solemn oath in blood and puts it in writing in the presence of lawyers that he will do what he said.

The oath or covenant aims to give the peasant double assurance that half of the kingdom is already his. He then demands that all the peasant needs to do to enjoy his benevolence is to believe him. In other words, God's covenants are not parity covenants like human covenants based on equal obligations and benefits. They are grace covenants.

In our text today, we begin to see another disclosure of God about Himself: He is a covenant-making God. He operates through covenants. A covenant is a solemn, formal agreement or pact between two or more individuals to carry out specific agreed-upon stipulations. There are generally two kinds of covenants in the Bible, those involving two or more humans coming together to make oaths or promises and those involving God and one or more humans.

In the former, covenants between two or more humans, both parties usually have specific obligations they must fulfill to be faithful to the Covenant. There were equal responsibilities and benefits. Failure to do their parts would lead to curses or even death. Blood covenants were usually dissolvable only by the death of the parties.

Regarding the latter, covenants between God and humans are covenants of grace. God makes the promises, initiates the covenant to anchor the souls of men, powers its fulfillment, and grants humanity the benefit.

Look at Hebrews 6:13-19, "When God made his promise to Abraham, since there was no one greater for him to swear by, he swore by himself...People swear by someone greater than themselves, and the oath confirms what is said and puts an end to all argument. Because God wanted to make the unchanging nature of his purpose very clear to the heirs of what was promised, he confirmed it with an oath.

God did this so that, by two unchangeable things in which God can't lie, we who have fled to take hold of the hope set before us may be greatly encouraged. We have this hope as an anchor for the soul, firm and secure. It enters the inner sanctuary behind the curtain,"

The Bible is a record of God's covenants with man. That is why it is divided into two sections: the old and new Testaments. "Testament" is another word for covenant. It tells the story of the initiation of God's covenants, the promises attached to them, and the outworking of the covenants in the lives of those that were the beneficiaries.

The Old Testament mainly tells the story of Abraham's covenant and its outworking in the life of his natural descendants, the nation of Israel. The New Testament picks up the story and tells how the Abrahamic covenant became upgraded with an addition of a spiritual component and then made available to all the families of the earth through the sacrifice of Jesus. "But in fact the ministry Jesus has received is as superior to theirs as the covenant of which he is mediator is superior to the old one since the new covenant is established on better promises." (Hebrews 8:6).

How do all these apply to your life? You are an heir of a covenant. God has made promises to you in the Bible that He has bound Himself to fulfill to you by the shed blood of Jesus if you exercise faith in them. These promises were provided by grace, not because of your works or because you deserve them.

They are promises from a benevolent God who loves you enough to swear in blood to help your faith so you can believe and receive their fulfillment. His promises cover every aspect of your life (1 Peter 1:3, 4).

There is salvation for your soul, healing for your body and mind, wholeness for your family, help in your career, and more. God's promises in the bible cover everything you are experiencing now and will experience throughout your life. It even covers your life in eternity. God will not break His covenant.

It is time for you to stop living in defeat. Let the blood of Jesus affect your thinking. It was shed for you. It is an oath from God to you. Whenever you take communion, you are celebrating that oath. Don't let ignorance, religion, and false teaching cheat you of what Jesus suffered to make available to you.

Don't be like Israel, who had the Promised Land given to them but refused to believe God choosing instead to believe the evil reports of the spies and then wasted away in the wilderness. Remember the exhortation of Hebrews 4:2, "For we also have had the good news proclaimed to us, just as they did; but the message they heard was of no value to them, because they did not share the faith of those who obeyed." It is time to put your faith In God's covenant.

Decision of the Day

I understand that God is a covenant-making God. He has made a covenant with me in Christ. It is a covenant of better promises that covers all my life. I will exercise faith in God's promises, knowing they are oaths sworn in blood. They can never fail.

| DAY 40

POSSIBILITIES IN UNITY

"But the Lord came down to look at the city and the tower the people were building. "Look!" he said. "The people are united, and they all speak the same language. After this, nothing they set out to do will be impossible for them! Come, let's go down and confuse the people with different languages. Then they won't be able to understand each other."

- Genesis 11:5-6 NLT

During the Second World War, the United States led an effort named "The Manhattan Project" to develop the first atomic bomb. The United Kingdom and Canada were also behind the action. The project's goal was to beat Hitler in developing nuclear weapons.

It was an extensive project that required the contributions of scientists, engineers, and others. Over 130,000 people were employed working at over 30 sites at the cost of over $2 billion. It was an unprecedented project that required tens of thousands to work together, spurred by the common goal of defeating the Nazis. It was accomplished. The aftermath was the bombing of Hiroshima and Nagasaki, the end of World War 2, and the beginning of a nuclear arms race that has since then left the possibility of the annihilation of the planet to the decisions of a few individuals.

Another project that humans embarked upon, previously thought of as impossible, was the Apollo program. This was the effort of the United States to be the first to land a man on the moon and to accomplish it within a decade. It employed over 400,000 people and utilized the support of over 20,000 firms and universities at the cost of 24 billion dollars. Even though this was the most complicated and hazardous journey humanity had ever embarked upon, spurred on by unity of focus to achieve space superiority, it was accomplished in 1969, when Neil Armstrong became the first man to walk on the moon.

These two examples of human projects, among many, accomplished by unity of focus and a strong motivation, are in line with God's statement in our text today about the man He created, that when united, whatever they set out to do will not be held back from them. Through unity and collaboration, humans can accomplish incredible feats. This is an ability God placed in man so that man can carry out His purpose on the earth and for the whole of creation. It is part of the expression of the dominion God gave man at his creation. In our text, God respected that ability.

ORDER FROM CHAOS

Now, though this is a God-given ability, the problem comes when man tries to use this ability for a purpose that is contrary to God's or in rebellion with God, as in our text. They were united among themselves but not with God. When this takes place, the outcomes can be very disastrous. Therefore, God intervened in this case to stop them. God was not afraid or jealous of what they could accomplish. He was concerned for them and the consequences of their accomplishment, so He intervened to save man from himself.

You may find yourself drawn into many projects or endeavors in life. Some visions will come into your heart, or others will share with you, asking for your participation and support that may seem huge and impossible. Don't get scared at how daunting things may look. Your primary responsibility should be to find out if God is in the project because if it is conceived in God, it is achievable.

Also, recognize that there is power in unity. In any of your projects, don't try to do it alone. Pray God to send you people who will stand and work in agreement with you. When people come together around any purpose, there is the power to accomplish much. Still, when they come together around God's purpose and with God's backing, the experience is multiplied, and success is assured.

Decision of the Day

I understand there is power in uniting with others around God's purpose. It is my decision today to engage the

ORDER FROM CHAOS

help of others in my God-given vision. I will not be daunted by seemingly impossible dreams and goals in my path to fulfilling God's purpose for my life because, with God, all things are possible.

MEET THE GREATEST PERSON ALIVE!

I want to share with you the most crucial decision ever. Jesus came to the earth to live and die so that you might have life and live life abundantly, but the devil also has come to steal, kill, and destroy. Winning or losing in life depends on whose lordship you are under, either Jesus or the devil.

Romans 10:9 says that if you confess Jesus as Lord with your mouth and believe in your heart that God raised Him from the dead, you will be saved. You can yield your life over to the Lord Jesus Christ by saying this simple prayer:

"*Lord Jesus, I acknowledge that I'm a sinner. I believe that you came to the earth to die for my sins, and you rose from the dead to give me life abundantly. I confess you as Lord of my life. I ask you to come into my heart and make me a brand-new person. Amen.* If you just prayed this prayer and meant it, Jesus has come into your life and made you a brand-new person. He has delivered you from the authority of the devil and has given you dynamic power to live life abundantly. "

We want to know your decision so we can stand with you in prayer and send you faith-building materials to help you walk with God.

WE'D LOVE TO HEAR FROM YOU!

Let us know how this book has been a blessing to you. For more information about Gregory Lan Ijiwola's ministry or to contact Gregory about meetings and to give him feedback on this book, follow @pastorlan on Instagram, Twitter, or Facebook.

More Books by the Author

Just Before You Say I Do: A Roadmap for Singles

Mission Possible: Finding and Fulfilling your Life's Assignment

Irresistible Influence: You Can Also Make a Difference

The 21 Immutable Laws of Relationships: Follow Them, Win Friends and Influence People

The C.H.O.I.C.E Matrix: A Practical Guide to Choosing a Marriage Partner

Bibliography

1. Lucado, Max. *A Gentle Thunder: Hearing God Through the Storm.* Nashville: Thomas Nelson, 1995

www.ingramcontent.com/pod-product-compliance
Lightning Source LLC
LaVergne TN
LVHW051601070426
835507LV00021B/2709